WHERE
MIRACLES
HAPPEN

Also by Joan Wester Anderson

WHERE ANGELS WALK
True Stories of Heavenly Visitors

WHERE MIRACLES HAPPEN

True Stories of
Heavenly Encounters

JOAN WESTER ANDERSON

Brett Books, Inc.
Brooklyn, New York

Published in the United States of America by Brett Books, Inc., P.O. Box 290-637, Brooklyn, New York 11229-0011.

Library of Congress Cataloging-in-Publication Data

Anderson, Joan Wester.
    Where miracles happen : true stories of heavenly encounters / Joan Wester Anderson. — 1st ed.
       p.   cm.
    Includes bibliographical references.
       ISBN 0-9636620-1-5 (alk. paper)
       1. Angels—Case studies. 2. Miracles—Case studies. I. Title.
    BL477.A53 1994
    291.2'11—dc20   94-878

First Edition
Manufactured in the United States of America
Printed on acid-free paper

94   95   96   97   98   99   10   9   8   7   6   5   4   3

Book design by C. Linda Dingler

To my husband, children, and grandchild.
To my mother, brother, and sisters.
And to Barbara Brett, mentor and soul mate—
—You are the miracles in my life

As much of heaven is visible as we have eyes to see.
WILLIAM WINTER

Acknowledgments

I would like to thank those who so generously assisted me in my research and writing efforts.

I appreciate the information provided by the Reverend Andrew M. Greeley, Professor of Social Science, and the staff at the National Opinion Research Center (NORC) at the University of Chicago; Maureen Quinn of the Gallup Organization, Princeton, New Jersey; Donna Jarvis of the copyright office at Word Music, Irving, Texas; Sharon Smith, Resources Coordinator at Breakthrough Ministries, Lincoln, Virginia; Ann Shields of Renewal Ministries in Ann Arbor, Michigan; and authors Charles and Frances Hunter.

Helpful research departments at the Christian Broadcasting Network and *Guideposts* magazine deserve mention. The Islamic Information Center of America, the Asher Library at Spertus College of Judaica, The Compassionate Friends, the Swedenborg Foundation, and various studies conducted by the Department of Sociology and Anthropology at Purdue University provided valuable background material.

A special word of thanks must go to Kathleen Choi, columnist for the *Hawaii Catholic Herald,* John Ronner, author of *Do You Have a Guardian Angel?*, Gustav Niebuhr of *The Wall Street Journal*, and Andrea Gross, fellow member of the American Society of Journalists and Authors, as well as reporters from newspapers across the country, who freely shared their research.

I appreciate the technical information contributed by Tom Skilling, meteorologist at WGN Radio in Chicago; Christine Z. Pundy, M.D., ophthalmologist, Arlington Heights, Illinois; and Lieutenant Thomas P. Anderson of the Chicago Fire Department. The editors who published my letter asking for miracle experiences, especially those at *Writers Information Network, Liguorian, Women & Money, Leaves, Chicago Parent,* and *Home Times* deserve mention.

Most special are the friends who affirmed and encouraged me, as well as hundreds of readers who sent both stories and comments, a rich source of material for the following pages. May we all continue our search for God, remembering, in the words of Henri Nouwen, that "the closer we come to Him, the closer we come to one another."

J. W. A.
Arlington Heights, Illinois

Contents

CONTENTS

BOOK TWO: *ANGEL MIRACLES*

BOOK THREE: *MIRACLES FROM BEYOND*

CONTENTS

CONTENTS

~∾~

THE BEGINNING

Prologue

He walks with me and He talks with me,
And He tells me I am His own . . .

"IN THE GARDEN," TRADITIONAL SONG

Shortly after our family bought a house in Chicago's northwest suburbs in September 1971, I met Lynne Gould. She
appeared at the door one morning, accompanied by several
small sons, to welcome us to the neighborhood. I invited her
in, but she took one look at the boxes marked *Fragile—China*
still stacked on my floors, and declined (which endeared her to
me right away).

The Goulds lived directly behind us, our deep yards separated by a tall hedge with an opening in it, which we used
as a gate. I loved all the neighbors, but Lynne was special.
Immediately we sensed a bond and found ourselves cutting
past surface chatter and delving more deeply into each other's
feelings and beliefs.

Few topics were out of bounds for us, but spirituality was a
particular favorite. We discovered that, although we were both
Catholic, our faith attitudes differed. Lynne seemed relaxed,
confident in God's tender care, His willingness to get personally

involved in her daily life. Me? As one philosopher has said, the longest distance anyone travels is the twelve inches from the head to the heart. I tended to be dutiful, a bit scrupulous, and hard on myself. Although I had never thought of God as harsh or frightening, it was difficult to believe that His love for me was truly unconditional. As for miracles, they happened to saints, not ordinary people like me.

We had lived in our house for just a few weeks when autumn leaves began falling. Actually, they *rained* down, thickly covering our quarter acre. I collected lawn bags, and one afternoon when the children were in school, I went into the yard to rake.

The warm, sunlit day was delightful, but I made little headway. At the end of an hour, I had stuffed six bags, but there were several huge piles of leaves waiting, and half the yard remained untouched. Home ownership was losing its charm. I leaned on the rake for a moment, pushed the hair back from my eyes— and the world seemed to stop. There were no rings on my left hand. My diamond engagement ring and wedding band—not removed since our marriage—were gone.

Just then Lynne stepped through the hole in the hedge. Although she was at least fifty feet from me, she must have seen the shock on my face. "What's the matter?" she called.

"My rings—they're missing!" I could barely speak. I had lost a little weight during our move, and they must have slipped off somehow. But when? Where?

Lynne waded across the lawn to me. "When was the last time you saw them?" she asked.

Frantically I searched my memory, examining all the small, ordinary things I'd done that day. Making breakfast for the children, loading the washing machine—how often we glance at our hands without really seeing them. But I was sure I would have noticed missing rings during earlier tasks.

"They must have fallen off out here," I told Lynne, surveying the landscape with a sinking heart. How could we find anything in all that debris? I would never see the rings again. And not only were they uninsured, they were *loved*, irreplaceable. . . . Tears filled my eyes.

Lynne was more practical. "Let's pray about it," she said, and she knelt right down in the middle of the leaves. And, because she had hold of my hand, so did I.

"God," Lynne began without preamble, "we've got a problem here. . . ." Briefly she outlined the situation.

Despite my agitation, I felt a little embarrassed. What if a neighbor looked out and saw us praying—in public! Yet I was fascinated too. Lynne was talking to God with easy familiarity, as if He was her *real* Father, Someone who cared so much about her that He would be interested in anything she told Him. *Well, why not?* I thought suddenly. *I'm a parent, and there's nothing my children could need that I wouldn't provide.* If I was truly His child, wouldn't it work the same way?

Lynne was finishing her discussion. "We need a miracle, God," I heard her say. "Please let us find the rings." She sat back on her heels, wordlessly surveying the yard. Not for a moment did I assume God would actually do anything about her request. But Lynne had been dear to stand by.

As I watched, however, her eyes traveled across the orange and yellow piles. Slowly she stood up and walked past several deep mounds. When she reached one on the other side of the yard, she stopped, bent over, plunged her hand into it, and then straightened. "Here they are," she said, looking into her palm. "Here are your rings."

I probably screamed before I went running across to her. But there *both* rings were, unmistakably mine. We looked at each other, our faces wreathed in grins. "How did you—?" I hardly knew what to ask.

She laughed. "I didn't. God did it. I just kind of knew where to look."

"But that's impossible. . . ."

"Not really," she pointed out simply. "We asked for a miracle, didn't we?"

Something great seemed to tremble in the air, something awesome and wondrous. Was this what it meant to trust? Like two little girls, we had approached our Father, placed a broken toy in His lap, and asked with complete assurance (at least on Lynne's part), "Daddy, fix it."

Why should I have been surprised when He did?

What Are Miracles?

A miracle is a wonder, a beam of supernatural power injected into history. . . . [It] makes an opening in the wall that separates this world and another.

TIME, DECEMBER 30, 1991

A 1989 Gallup poll discovered that 83% of Americans believe in miracles, mainly because such events suggest that God exists and loves us, and that our lives have a purpose. But the finding of the rings in my backyard deepened my interest in the subject. What is a miracle? I wondered. How do we know when one happens?

According to Webster's Unabridged Dictionary, Encyclopedic Edition, a miracle is "an event or effect that apparently contradicts known scientific law, and is hence thought to be due to supernatural causes." Whether elaborate or unadorned, most miracles are *positive* happenings, occurring unexpectedly and usually outside the realm of ordinary life. "If you can explain it," says Betty Malz, author of *Angels Watching Over Me,* "it is not a miracle." Nor are miracles haphazard. The recipient usually has a sense of God's deliberate intervention, a change, an *answer.*

Among the world's many religions, we find different responses to miracles. For example, the Catholic Church accepts their existence, but only when the event defies the known laws of science. And claims are not easily verified. A case in point is the shrine at Lourdes in France. Although there have been thousands of purported divine healings there, only 65 have made it through the stringent procedures of the International Medical Commission to be officially declared miracles. Since 1981, millions of people have witnessed extraordinary events at Medjugorje in the former Yugoslavia, but the Church is still investigating the situation without official comment, and will probably do so for years to come.

Protestant denominations differ on miracles. Some believe that Jesus healed the sick, multiplied food, commanded the sea to be silent only for the purpose of establishing his church on earth, and then such heaven-directed wonders stopped. Martin Luther originally denied the possibility of divine healings as well as other miracles, though he later changed his mind. John Calvin, in *Institutes of the Christian Religion*, wrote that such gifts "vanished in order to make the preaching of the Gospel marvelous forever."

However, a 1987 document from Fuller Theological Seminary, entitled "Ministry and the Miraculous," affirms what a growing number of denominations now accept, that God does work miraculously today, although "we must be transparently ready to submit our claims . . . to the most rigorous of empirical testing," to guard against charlatans and hoaxes.

This view is also accepted by more charismatic Christians. "In this age of skepticism, I often hear people say, 'But God isn't working miracles anymore,' " writes Harald Bredesen, pastor and author of *Need a Miracle?*. "I've got news for them—good news. God isn't working miracles any less!" Perhaps people block the availability of miracles, or the answers to any prayers, for that matter, says Bredesen, "by consciously or unconsciously thinking of God in too small terms, of considering Him in terms of our own human limitations."

Jews believe in miracles too. "God is not subject to the laws He established for his universe," according to Rabbi Simon Greenberg, writing in *A Jewish Philosophy and Pattern of Life.* "He remains their unchallenged master, who can manipulate them at will."

However, one's faith must not *depend* on the miraculous, cautions Rabbi Jack Riemer, president of the Greater Miami Rabbinical Association. "Miracles are the frosting on the cake, but, as my wife, Sue, says, we have to bake the cake first!" he adds with a smile. "We can pray for them, but we're supposed to act, work, and do as if they didn't exist." (Most Christian leaders would agree.) More practically, Jews prefer to concentrate on "the miracles that are daily with us," the blessings of the beautiful in the commonplace.

The Islamic view is similar. "Miracles are given by the grace of Allah, the only God, not through our own power," says Dr. Musa Qutub, president of the Islamic Information Center of America. "We can ask for anything, because anything is possible." And it is in the asking that our faith grows. "No one who raises his hand to Allah ever comes back empty," Dr. Qutub explains.

Can we "prove" miracles? Usually not. Even if the circumstances seem astonishing, in the end many must be left to the observer to decide. But sometimes we recognize one by our reaction—perhaps a tiny quiver in the pit of our stomach, a chill running through us, a prick of tears, or our heart lifting in wordless response. Miracles can also be identified in hindsight by the positive, often profound changes they make in our lives.

My own "miracle of the rings" changed me. Gradually, I

grew more willing to ask for spiritual help and seek God's plan for me, less fearful of being considered "unworthy." Still, it wasn't until I wrote my eighth book, *Where Angels Walk*, in 1992, that a new door to understanding miracles opened to me. People were so moved by the true stories of others who were rescued, consoled, or touched in a special way by an angel that they willingly shared their own heavenly experiences with me. (Some requested anonymity, and are denoted here with an asterisk [*].) Most wrote in response to my book, or spoke to me after I had given a talk. Others called radio shows where I was a guest, usually over the telephone.

It was a touching experience, sitting quietly in my home office, sometimes late at night, connecting with people all over the country who were willing to publicly discuss their angel encounters. Or seeing the dawning awareness of God's love on the face of a stranger who approached my book-signing table, or tentatively opened his heart in an airport waiting room. Every day brought stories of sorrow turned into joy, of lives filled with reawakenings, of searches that had ended, as all good searches do, in the arms of the Father.

Some of these encounters came through angels, others through loved ones already in paradise. Answers to prayers, unexplained healings, the wonders of nature . . . occasionally a story contained more than one spiritual ingredient, making it harder to categorize, but even more enjoyable to hear. Most illuminating, God seemed to be at work not just at shrines but *everywhere*. The greatest and most profound adventures with Him were taking place, not at the feet of distant gurus, but in our own kitchens, our cars, our prayer communities, wherever hearts were open enough to whisper, "Come, Lord, come. . . ."

Gradually I realized that such happenings were far too precious to hide in my files. As I read them and heard them, it became clear that I would have to share many of them in another book, one not only about angels, but also about faith and love . . . and, yes, about miracles. The groundwork God had so lovingly laid in my backyard was finally bearing fruit.

BOOK ONE

⁓⁓

MIRACLES THROUGH PRAYER

The Power of Prayer

It may never be mine,
The loaf or the kiss or the kingdom
Because of beseeching;
But I know that my hand
Is an arm's length nearer the sky
For reaching.

EDWIN QUARLES, "*PETITION*"

*J*anice Stiehler of Baldwin, New York, worried when the night Yankees game her teenage son was attending went into extra innings. Now Kurt and his friends would have to take the subway to Penn Station very late at night.

Janice went to sleep, but at precisely one-ten A.M., she awoke to the crash of a shattered windowpane, as if someone was breaking into the house. Frightened, she roused her husband and they both searched everywhere. But they found no evidence of burglars and no broken glass. Nor had Kurt come home. "For some reason, I felt compelled to pray for him," Janice recalls. She sat in the kitchen, prayed—and waited.

An hour later, a Penn Station security officer phoned. The boys had been horsing around at the terminal, and Kurt's arm had crashed through a huge storefront window. The broken-glass pieces were so jagged and heavy that the arm should have been completely severed, the amazed officer explained. But Kurt had sustained no injury, not even a scratch.

"When did this happen?" Janice asked.

"One-fifteen," came the answer.

Then Janice understood. She had been awakened just in time to pray for Kurt. And somehow, across the miles, her prayers had protected him.

When situations work out, we often assume it's a coincidence or the result of our own efforts. And sometimes it is. But answers also come because we pray.

Prayer is most commonly defined as the raising of our minds and hearts to God. We can praise and adore God, express sorrow for an action we regret, give thanks, ask for help. Prayer covers the complete spectrum of human emotion—from grief to anger to wonder. It can arise from specific occasions, or flow casually, like a chat with a good friend. Ideally, prayer "takes no time but it occupies all our time," says Quaker author Thomas Kelly. "[It is] a gentle receptiveness to divine breathings."

Americans are a prayerful people. Three-quarters of us claim to pray at least once a week, and 52% pray daily.[1] Years ago, I told a friend that I wished I had time to pray. She looked at me. "I don't have time *not* to pray," she said. I discovered that she was right. Once I made prayer my first priority, God provided all the time I required for everything else, at least everything that *He* wanted me to accomplish!

But is it necessary to pray? If God already knows what we need, why doesn't He just give it to us? "[Prayer] is certainly not to nag God into doing what He is reluctant to do, nor to earn the favors that He gives us," says George Martin, a leader in the Catholic Charismatic Renewal. "God does not have to be talked into loving us."

Instead, prayer seems to be necessary for *our* welfare, to place us in an intimate relationship with our Creator, to fill the God-shaped vacuum within us that will never be satisfied with anything but God. "The value of persistent prayer is not that God will hear us," observed historian William McGill, "but that we will finally hear God."

Sometimes we have misconceptions about prayer. We decide our own agenda, then ask God to bless it. When He doesn't, we conclude that He didn't answer our prayer. But He did. He said "no," because what we asked was not in our best interest. It's similar to a mother who took her toddler on a shopping trip. Little Joey saw a toy he wanted. The toy was poorly made, and Mom knew it would soon break and disappoint him. The following week was also Joey's birthday, and she had hidden a shiny red tricycle, which would delight him far more than the cheap plaything he thought he wanted.

When Mom refused to buy the toy, however, Joey threw a tantrum. Like us, he didn't understand that his parent had a larger view of his life—and something better in store.

A more effective way to pray is to trust God's love for us and surrender the direction of our life to Him. The late author Catherine Marshall once noted that "God absolutely refuses to violate our free will; therefore, unless self-will is voluntarily given up, God cannot move to answer prayer." She found that whenever she stopped arguing and instead said, "Okay, God, whatever You want," exciting answers came.

We can pray alone or united with others, in group worship or a shared purpose. The First Baptist Church of Fort Lauderdale, Florida, is one of a growing number of congregations using the Watchman program, in which four volunteers per hour, in their homes, intercede for our nation. While praying, each faces a different direction, like guardians. (This is taken from Isaiah 62:6: "I have posted watchmen on your walls, O Jerusalem; they will never be silent day or night.")

Many people attest to feeling supported, even *carried,* when others petition God for them during a difficult time. "I don't know how I would have gotten through without prayer," they say. And it's true.

Have you ever cried out: "Why me, God? Why must I suffer? Why did someone I love die? Why have my efforts failed?" It's difficult to understand why there is pain in our world, why prayers seem to go unheard. Perhaps God is waiting for *us* to heal one another's wounds. Or perhaps our vision is limited. "On earth we see only the back of the tapestry," all the seemingly random threads and knots, said Dutch missionary Corrie ten Boom. "But the time will come when we will behold the front in all its amazing beauty." In the end, it will all make sense.

Until that time, we can hold tightly to God's hand through prayer, as people in the following stories did. They learned that no job is too difficult, no heartache too devastating, no life ever barren—with God.

A Promise on Mother's Day

Something happens when we pray,
Take our place and therein stay,
Wrestle on 'til break of day;
Ever let us pray.

ANONYMOUS

Sue and Kenny Burton had tried for more than two years to have a baby, and things weren't going well. Month after month, despite many medical tests, they continued to be disappointed. People in their tiny, close-knit town of Frankfort, Kansas, knew about the Burtons' dream and were praying for them.

At that time, Sue was singing contemporary Christian songs in a sextet formed by women from Frankfort's United Methodist Church. The group, ironically named Special Delivery, performed regularly at mother-daughter banquets, Elk and Moose club meetings and other functions. "Usually during a program we would each share a little personal history with the audience," Sue explains. "Since we ranged from teenage to grandmother status, people could relate to all of us."

The other singers, knowing Sue's longing for a baby, encouraged her to share that with audiences too, and she did. The response was tremendously supportive. After the Christmas concerts, many people came up to assure Sue that they would add their prayers to those of her neighbors. In March, a woman from South Dakota even predicted that at this time next year, Sue would have a baby daughter. Although Sue and Kenny seemed no closer to decorating a nursery, it helped to know so many people cared.

On Mother's Day weekend, Sue drove her mother to Kansas City to spend some time with Sue's sister, Shelley, who attended college there. The three visited shopping malls all day Saturday, and Sue conscientiously pressed the automatic door lock every time they parked and got out of her car. "We joked about being overly cautious in the Big City, but there was no point in being careless," Sue says.

Sunday morning, the trio awakened to a steady rain. They lounged around in Shelley's apartment and had an early lunch. The downpour continued, so eventually the three decided to go out, anyway. Dodging raindrops, they splashed across the parking lot to Sue's car. "Hurry up! I'm getting soaked!" Shelley laughed as Sue unlocked the driver's door, then pressed the switch to open the other doors.

Shelley scrambled into the front seat, while their mother got in back. "Look at this!" she exclaimed as her daughters turned around. On the backseat was a pink baby bootie.

"Where did that come from?" Sue asked. "It wasn't there yesterday, was it, Mom?"

"No," her mother said. "I was in and out of here all day, and I never saw it."

"Could it have been stuck down in the seat, maybe left by one of your friends in Frankfort?" Shelley wondered.

Sue shook her head. "I doubt it. My friends' children are all older. I don't think a baby has ever been in this car."

The women pondered over that awhile.

"Someone must have found it lying near the car just now and tossed it in, thinking it was ours," Shelley tried again.

"But," Sue pointed out, "the car was never open—you know I've locked the doors whenever we got out. And why would anyone think a bootie belonged to us? No one here knows us."

"Look how muddy and wet it is outside," Sue's mother added. "But this bootie is clean and dry."

The women fell silent again, turning over possible explanations in their minds. But no solution emerged. The bootie's position looked *deliberate,* as if someone had wanted to be sure it was seen.

"What if. . . ?" Sue couldn't finish her sentence. But the others knew what she was thinking. Was the bootie a message from heaven, a sign that all those prayers ascending from the Kansas plains were about to be answered?

Sue hardly dared to hope. She took the bootie home, put it in her Bible, and waited. Waited until she realized she was indeed pregnant, had been pregnant on that Mother's Day morning, and would, just as the lady from South Dakota predicted, be a mother—of a daughter—very soon. "When people asked how I could be so sure of a girl, I would simply show them the bootie," Sue says. "Would God send pink for any other reason?"

Today, five years later, the bootie hangs over Paige Elizabeth Burton's bed as a constant reminder that God answers prayers. In fact, He answers in abundance, for Paige now has a little sister. "I have no doubt that an angel left the bootie there as a sign for me," Sue says.

For Sue, every day is Mother's Day.

Answer in the Wind

I like to compare prayer to the wind. You cannot actually see the wind, but you can see the results of it.

ROSALIND RINKER, *HOW TO HAVE FAMILY PRAYERS*

*I*t was a raw January day as the bus left Benton, Wisconsin, but Dick Wilson* barely noticed. Dick had just attended his mother's funeral. Although she'd had severe diabetes for many years and it was a relief to see her suffering end, his heart was still heavy.

When the summons had come, Dick planned to drive to Wisconsin from his home in Sedona, Arizona. But the weather in that mountainous area was treacherous, and even worse conditions had been predicted. Instead, his wife, Nancy,* had driven him to the Phoenix airport where he boarded a plane.

Now he was on his way back to Nancy and the six of their ten children who still lived with them. It would have been more convenient to fly back, but the bus fare would be easier on the family budget.

Miles rolled by. Dick was cold and sorrowful, and the trip seemed endless. Finally, in the middle of the night, the bus pulled into the terminal in Tucumcari, New Mexico, for his last transfer. There was time for a quick snack, so Dick went into a nearby restaurant. Lost in thought, he was startled when a driver yelled from the door: "Phoenix bus is leaving, folks. Last call to board."

Last call! Dick got up, grabbed his jacket, then reached inside his shirt pocket for his ticket. But his pocket was empty. Quickly Dick checked the rest of his possessions. Yes, here was his wallet, his comb and coins. . . . But as he inspected the floor and even the chair he'd been sitting on, his pulse began to race. His ticket was gone.

What was he going to do? He had no cash for another ticket. Perhaps he had dropped it on the bus. Panic building, Dick ran to the terminal lot. People were boarding the Phoenix bus, but he dashed to the one he had just ridden. A man was sweeping it out.

"Have you found a ticket?" Dick asked the workman.

"Nope." The workman paused and looked around at the little pile of cigarette butts and candy wrappers. "There's nothing here but this junk."

"Oh, God, please help me. . . ." Dick stepped down from the bus, his head swimming. Now what? He set out down the street, away from the restaurant. If only he hadn't been so careless, so absorbed in his own grief! How could he have done something so stupid?

The wind was blowing strongly, and as Dick trudged, head down, debris whirled past. Rubbish blew against him, and, blindly, Dick hit out at it, grabbing one troublesome piece of paper to crumple it in frustration. He'd have to phone Nancy, have her wire some money out of their tight budget. And in the meantime the bus would leave. How long would he be stuck here?

Turning, Dick retraced his steps past the terminal and back

to the restaurant. As he pushed the door open, he realized that his fist was still closed around that crushed piece of wastepaper. Absently, he glanced at it before tossing it aside.

It was his missing ticket.

Dick reached home safely, and has never forgotten the wonder of that answered prayer.

Vital Signs

I never spoke with God,
Nor visited in heaven;
Yet certain am I of the spot
As if the chart were given.

EMILY DICKINSON, *POEMS*

 W hen Emily Weichman was seven months old, she had a stroke. Although the episode had never been repeated, Emily was still delicate, and her mother, Marlene, watched her carefully for signs of illness or distress. So did the members of the Weichmans' church community, St. Paul Lutheran in West Point, Nebraska. "Emily has many adoptive grandparents," Marlene says. "Everyone is concerned about her."

In September 1991, Marlene, her husband, and Emily, then five, decided to accompany Marlene's parents to Seattle to visit relatives. On the way home, they stayed overnight at a campsite in Yellowstone National Park.

The following morning Emily seemed lethargic, and after they got on the road she quickly fell asleep again. The family was driving through a desolate stretch of Wyoming when Emily abruptly awoke.

"Mommy," she said, "I'm sick." Marlene looked at her

daughter. Emily's eyes seemed out of focus, shifting to the right. A moment later she started vomiting.

They had just driven over some road oil. Were fumes nauseating Emily? Marlene's father stopped the RV, and everyone walked her up and down. She was conscious and apparently aware, but Marlene, a teacher, had had epileptic students, and she felt a chill of apprehension. Emily's symptoms seemed ominously similar. "Dad," she said, "we've got to get Emily to a hospital right away!"

The nearest town, Rock Springs, was over sixty miles away. Marlene's father sped off, and everyone began to pray.

Twenty miles, thirty. . . . The scenery flew by, but not quickly enough. Emily seemed to be fading. Everyone kept praying, but as they approached Rock Springs, they could see that the town below was far larger than they had anticipated. There would certainly be a hospital here, but how would they find it? Precious moments would be lost as they searched. Emily was unconscious now. "Lord," Marlene whispered as she held her daughter tightly, "we need to find a doctor fast."

Just as they approached an interstate highway, everyone saw a blue marker with a white *H* on it—a hospital sign! Thank God! Soon they saw another. At least four signs formed a reassuring blue-and-white trail, which Marlene's father followed on and off the interstate, right to the hospital.

An emergency-room physician diagnosed Emily's condition as a mild epileptic seizure, did a CAT scan and quickly stabilized her with anticonvulsant drugs.

Only afterward, as Emily rested safely in her room, did Marlene feel the full impact of the crisis. "If it weren't for those hospital signs," she told the physician, "we might still be driving around."

The doctor looked at her curiously. "What signs?"

"The ones lining our route," Marlene explained. "They were

literally a lifesaver—we couldn't have found the hospital without them."

The doctor was perplexed. "I live about eight miles out on that road. I travel it every day here," he told her. "I've never seen any hospital signs."

Marlene didn't know what to think. All four adults in the van had seen the markers. But her father and her husband were now at a gas station they had passed on the way in, having the RV checked out. When they returned, she'd ask them.

The men returned late—because they had gotten lost. "We were counting on those blue-and-white signs to guide us," her father said. "But they were gone."

Still perplexed, Marlene phoned the Rock Springs Chamber of Commerce the next day. But an official could provide no explanation. "There have never been any hospital signs along that route," he said.

With the help of anticonvulsant drugs, Emily is stable and happy today, and considered a "miracle child" among the members of St. Paul, many of whom make it a point to travel that same road whenever they can. There's no doubt it's holy ground.[2]

Deliverance
from the Depths

Here's a test to find whether your mission on earth is
finished: If you're alive, it isn't.

RICHARD BACH,
AUTHOR OF *JONATHAN LIVINGSTON SEAGULL*

*I*n April 1993, Don Spann and John Thomson pulled out
of the Charleston, South Carolina, harbor on Don's forty-six-
foot boat, *Perseverance,* for a routine two-day cruise to Fort
Lauderdale, Florida.

By the middle of the second day, however, clouds had rolled
in and the ocean was rough. John T. manned the helm while
Don sat in the back. Ironically, although Don stresses safety
constantly to his employees at his company, Span-America, his
life vest was beside him on the seat.

The boat dipped and bounced. Don had just gotten to his
feet when it smacked against an especially high wave. Off
balance, he cartwheeled over the side, hit the swim platform,
and plunged into the ocean.

Perseverance had already passed when Don surfaced. Frantically, he whistled, waved his arms, and yelled. "John T.!

I'm here! Turn around!" But the craft continued on, John T. facing forward and unaware of Don's fall. Don watched it for five or six more waves, listened to the motor a little longer. Then silence descended. It was the loneliest sound he had ever heard.

Surely John T. would discover his absence right away, and return! Don scanned the horizon, remembering his Marine Corps training to fight panic, and waited. But ten minutes passed, and nothing happened.

What was he going to do? The ocean temperature was low enough to cause hypothermia if he didn't keep moving. But how long could he tread water? And would his movements cause a cramp or, worse, attract marlins or sharks? What if he drowned, or was mauled by fish and washed ashore later? How would his family deal with such a trauma?

He removed his shoes, attempting to use them as flotation aids, but they only became waterlogged, and he let them float away. His breathing was more labored now, and it was harder to float on either his stomach or his back. Twenty minutes passed. Twenty-five. . . .

It had been a long time since Don had thought much about God. But now he prayed aloud. "God," he said as waves rolled over him, "You're using some drastic measures to get my attention. I'm sorry I haven't been smart enough to listen to You. But if You let me live, I'll fulfill Your mission for me, whatever that might be."

Then Don thought he heard a voice inside him. Was it God? No, this voice seemed seductive, even frightening. "Don," it whispered, "you're not going to get out of this situation. Why don't you relax and die peacefully?"

Don ignored the voice. But it came again, this time more insistent. "Give up, give up. . . . "

"No!" Don answered aloud. "I'm going to fight!" But how?

He had been in the water far too long, and he was colder, slower. Would he go under soon, for the last time?

"Let go, Don," the insidious voice pushed at him once more. "It would be so easy. . . ."

"I won't," Don said through clenched, chattering teeth. He knew he was being tempted, in death just as in life. But almost unconsciously he clung to a security he had known long ago. *God, be with me now,* he prayed. "I won't give up!" he shouted to the nameless enemy. "Even if I'm ten feet under!"

His voice echoed across the waves. Somehow he knew that the insidious voice had gone. He was alone again.

It had been almost an hour now, and slowly Don began to sink. At times he would think he was above the waves, only to open his eyes and realize he was under. That's why, at first, he wasn't sure he heard the engine noise. Then, as if in a dream, he spotted something moving toward him. It was just a few inches long at first . . . a boat, with a figure at the helm—John T., scanning the horizon with glasses! "I heard him elatedly shout my name, and I knew that he had seen me," Don says. "I think, just for a moment, I blacked out."

But John T.'s shout roused him. "Catch the line!"

Exhausted, Don reached for the rope, wrapping it around his arm because he was too weak to grasp it in his hand.

"I remember being pulled through the water and getting tangled up," Don says. He couldn't make it! But then he felt strong hands gripping his right bicep and right forearm, holding him up. *John T.!* Why had he gotten into the water? Who was manning the boat?

And now there was a *second* set of hands on his other side, gripping his left bicep and forearm. The hands seemed to push him, propelling him through that last impossible distance. Where had John T. found an extra person to help?

Somehow Don was under the swim ladder, and John T. was yelling at him: "Grab hold! Grab hold!"

But Don couldn't. His exhausted, frozen muscles refused to work anymore. He would drown here after all. . . . But then he felt firm hands underwater, placing his foot on the lowest rung. Firm palms pushed on his bottom. "Suddenly I was standing straight up on the ladder," he says. "And John T., who is fifty pounds lighter, flipped me around and dragged me in."

A Coast Guard helicopter eventually plucked Don from the *Perseverance* and took him to Jacksonville University Hospital, where he stayed for four days, being treated for the results of hypothermia. Only later did Don recall the strange events surrounding his rescue.

"John T.," he asked one day, "who else helped pull me into the boat?"

John T. frowned. "What are you talking about?"

"I know you were in the water with someone else, because I felt two sets of hands holding me up," Don explained. "In fact, I couldn't climb the ladder, and you both pushed me."

John T. wore a strange expression. "I was never in the water, Don," he said. "I pulled you in from the swim platform. And I was alone."

Today Don is healthy, and back at the helm of his boat and his life. "I'm not sure why I was spared from temptation and from death," he says. "But I sense that I am to pay attention and wait to be shown what I am to do." And while he waits, he gives thanks. To John T., for his skill and courage.

And to heavenly hands that came in answer to his prayers.

Perfect Timing

If our daily walk with the Lord is to be a close and intimate relationship, then we must share all things with Him, no matter how ordinary.

MARY MATHEWSON, A READER FROM ADA, OHIO

*H*ow do we know when God answers a prayer? Rarely does He communicate with trumpet blasts or skywriting. However, there are those moments when a response is so immediate, so explicit, that it couldn't be anyone *but* God. . . .

As a single parent, Debra Bredican struggled to raise a small daughter in a one-bedroom apartment in suburban Chicago. To supplement her salary, she made health-food dinners for friends. Her client base grew as satisfied customers spread the word about Debra's tasty menus.

Debra dreamed of expanding, but she would need a second bedroom for an office, plus an apartment manager who would let her install a second refrigerator. Both seemed impossible goals. She couldn't afford more than a $650 monthly rental—too modest for the area she had in mind. And buying a second refrigerator would take all her savings. Was it too risky? Debra talked it over with God. "If You want me to do this," she told Him, "You'll have to figure it out."

Soon Debra found an apartment complex in a perfect location. But the two-bedroom rents were too expensive. She kept looking—and praying—and occasionally checked back with the complex.

"You're in luck," the rental agent told her one day. "Because of renovations, we're lowering rents on all two-bedroom units for the next six months."

"How much will they be?" Debra scarcely dared to ask.

"Six hundred and fifty-two dollars," the agent answered.

Debra was *almost* convinced that this was God's answer. But there was one more thing. "I'm expanding my home business," she told the agent. "I'm going to need an apartment with two refrigerators."

"Two refrigerators?" The woman laughed. "That's just about impossible. But let me see what I can do."

Debra went home, almost afraid to hope. But the next day, the agent phoned. "This is odd, Debra," she began. "Remember I told you we're in the middle of a huge remodeling job?"

Debra remembered.

"Well, we ordered two hundred and twenty new refrigerators. Yesterday they delivered two hundred and twenty-one. It will be cheaper for us to put the extra in your apartment than to send it back."

Debra had no more doubts. Today her business is thriving, thanks to prayers answered at just the right time.

My nephew Tom Anderson also received a heavenly go-ahead. Tom is a cabinetmaker, and after working for others for several years, he decided to go solo. He wanted to do the kind of fine woodcrafting that satisfies him right down to his soul.

But searching for customers, meeting his overhead, and doing the work itself took more time than Tom had figured. He also grappled with tax forms, bookkeeping, and a slew of new responsibilities he neither wanted nor enjoyed. His dream was rapidly turning into an exhausting treadmill.

One morning as he sped along to an appointment, Tom found himself rethinking his plans. Had he made the right decision? He had prayed about it beforehand and felt sure that God approved, but now he was having second thoughts. "God, I'm overwhelmed," he sighed. "Should I go back to a safe nine-to-five job without all this worry? Please tell me what You want me to do."

Just then Tom passed a parked police car and realized with a sinking heart that he was going at least twenty-five miles over the speed limit. In his rearview mirror, he saw the car move out and flash its lights. Great. Tom pulled over and slumped dejectedly in the seat. Not only would he be even later to his appointment, he sure had his answer now. How much more negative a signal could God send?

"License and registration, please." The officer approached Tom's truck, ticket book in hand.

"Yes, sir." Tom didn't even put up a defense. He was so disappointed at the thought of giving up his goals that he barely glanced at the officer—until a moment or two had passed. Then he realized the officer was looking at his tools, stacked in the front seat because his new truck didn't yet have a cover.

The policeman gestured at them. "What do you do for a living?" he asked.

"I'm a cabinetmaker." Tom's curiosity mounted. What did this have to do with a traffic stop?

The officer handed Tom his license—without a ticket. "Go slower the next time," he said. "And wear your seat belt." Tom could hardly believe it. But the officer wasn't finished.

He leaned against Tom's truck. "I moonlight as a general contractor," he said. "And I've got sixteen custom kitchens and fifteen bathrooms that all need cabinets right now. Think you'd be interested?"

"It was a real answer, just what I had asked for," Tom says today as he runs his successful business. "God was saying 'Keep going—but slow down.' I know He'll always give me the directions I need."

Eighteen-year-old Marci Vance had an uncomfortable home situation. Things had always been painful between her and her adoptive father. Now he was demanding that she get a job and move out. "I was young and scared, and I hadn't landed anything yet," Marci explains. Tension grew.

Finally, Marci found a job, but it required her to wear gray slacks and a white blouse every day. She had enough money to buy the blouse, but not the slacks. And there was no use asking her father to help—he was already angry. "If you don't start working right away, you're out of here!" he told her one morning.

Marci felt completely abandoned. What would become of her if she was thrown out of her house? It was drizzling, and she walked aimlessly, letting the tears come. Eventually she sat down on a wall across from a school. *God, what am I going to do?* she prayed. *Please help me.*

A short time later, Marci glanced up—at a beautiful rainbow arcing across the sky. "A powerful peace came over me," she says. "I felt that I had nothing to worry about."

Heartened, she walked over to her Aunt Pam's house. Moments before Marci arrived, a friend of Pam's had stopped in to drop off some garments for Pam's church's clothing drive. "Marci, see if there's anything you want in that pile before I pack it," Pam suggested.

There was. Two pairs of attractive gray slacks that fit her perfectly.

"I get frustrated that my writing career isn't where I'd like it to be," says Sue Markgraf, who works full-time and freelances on weekends around the demands of her young family. One cold, overcast Saturday morning, she sat staring blankly at the TV. The children were occupied, and there were notes on her computer for her next writing project. She really should get on with it.

But a combination of fatigue and discouragement kept her from moving. Were her efforts really leading her anywhere? Would she ever make a difference through her work?

Suddenly, as if in answer, an intense ray of light streamed through the window in front of her. It was brilliant, almost white, as if the very air itself were glowing from within. But how? The other windows still looked out on gray and gloom. Where was this light's source? "I wanted to shield my eyes and look away, but I couldn't," she says. "I shifted on the sofa, but the light seemed to follow me." This was no ordinary sunbeam.

Then, in the center of this radiance, Sue saw a shadowy figure. She was drawn to its warmth, compelled to watch it. Although she didn't hear actual words, she *felt* the figure speaking to her. "Go back to your story," it said. "Peace is coming."

Awed, Sue drank in the light. She felt unworthy of its presence, yet exalted at the same time. "I forced myself to continue looking, to continue feeling," she says, until the figure and the light shimmered, then faded away.

Sue still struggles with the meaning of that blissful vision. But she does feel more confident about her work and about God's plan for her, whatever it is. "I know there is a greater force that has an incredible investment in me," she says. "It pushes me constantly, yet it comforts me. I pray that it stays by my side always."

Kathy and Bill Colby were late for dinner at her sister's house. Hurried and preoccupied, Kathy laid her key ring on the roof of the car, then strapped their ten-month-old into his seat.

"Let's go!" Bill dashed out the front door and leaped into the driver's seat.

Kathy scooted into the passenger side, forgetting her keys, and they sped off. Approaching the expressway, they tore down the entrance ramp. Just then they heard something fly off the roof of the car and hit the pavement with a jangly crash. "What was that?" Bill asked.

"Oh, no! My keys!" Kathy was very upset. She works two part-time jobs, and all her business keys, as well as her house and car keys, were on the ring. While she explained, Bill drove sixty-five miles an hour.

"I'm going to get off at the next exit, go back, and drive down that entrance ramp again," he decided. "It's still light out—we can park and look for the keys."

When they returned to the ramp, Bill pulled onto the shoulder, got out, and walked ahead, looking near the curb. Kathy got out too and started searching in a wider arc. *What an evening!* she thought. They were late, she was going to have trouble duplicating all those keys, and now the baby was starting to cry. . . .

Tentatively Kathy looked up at the sky. "If Anyone can hear me . . ." she murmured, ". . . well, I need some help."

She glanced back at the baby, and froze, astonished. At that moment, Bill turned and saw the same thing. On the roof of the car sat her keys.

Impossible. The roof sloped, with no protective lip or rim. Both had heard the keys fall, and neither had seen anything on the roof when they got out of the car. Yet the keys were there, as if placed by a loving Parent—to whom no request was too small.

Doris Neill Johnson came out of her women's specialty store in Spencer, Iowa, into freezing temperatures and a sudden blizzard. Although night had not yet fallen, it was almost impossible to see because of a condition known as "whiteout." Doris drove a familiar shortcut route through a sparsely populated area, but the road was barely visible and she felt completely lost.

Soon she decided to abandon the car and walk. *It can't be more than a mile,* she told herself. *I'll be safer feeling my way on foot than possibly having a traffic accident.*

But just a few moments passed before Doris realized she had made a major mistake. It was getting dark, and the swirling snow blinded her, making her feel dazed and disoriented. Her light-gray coat blended with the landscape, and the snow was far deeper than she'd anticipated. What if she fell and hurt herself? In this deserted area, she could freeze before anyone saw her. "God, send help," Doris prayed aloud.

She took another few steps. It was hopeless—she could neither move nor see. Panic built within her. Then, "as if God was calling to me," she heard a man shouting.

"This way! Keep coming!"

Who was calling? Where was he?

"Here! Come, come!" The voice sounded as if it knew what it was doing.

Doris prayed for strength, and followed it.

"Turn right just a little . . . that's it, that's it," the voice went on. It was somewhat distorted by the wind, but at least she was no longer alone in this terrible night. "Come on now." He sounded closer.

Doris struggled, one painful step at a time, and at last she could see lamplight in the window of a house just ahead, and a man standing in an open doorway.

"You've done it!" the man called delightedly as she collapsed at the door.

The couple had already drawn their drapes against the windy drafts, they told Doris later. "We wouldn't have opened them again tonight, but, well ... it's strange," the man tried to explain. "We had this odd sudden impulse to look at the storm again." He had opened the drapes, thought he saw something moving—and called, just in case.

Doris didn't think it was odd at all. She had prayed, hadn't she?

Heavenly Mission

I used to ask God to help me.
Then I asked if I might help him.

James Hudson Taylor, missionary

*H*ave you ever felt a quickening in your spirit, a sense that you're being led, even pushed? Sometimes that's God answering a prayer, and using *you* to do it, if you're willing.

It was November 1990, and Daniel Sheridan was insulating the crawl space in the home he had just purchased. Tomorrow he could finish the job, and since New York City firefighters can swap duty hours with one another, Danny made a few calls and finally got John to work for him the next day.

But late that night, another buddy phoned Danny and asked if John could substitute for *him* instead. Danny protested, but eventually agreed, grumbling all the way.

He was still in a bad mood the next day when he reported for duty. "We started as usual, checking tools, washing the floors—it was pretty uneventful," Danny says. About noon, an alarm sounded on a blaze in an old wooden tenement three blocks from their firehouse. Danny recognized the address and assumed, as the others did, that it was probably one of the many false alarms they received every week.

When a false alarm is suspected, firefighters usually do not put on their heavier coats and helmets. But as Danny got dressed, he was conscious of an inner voice, a distinct prod. "Gear up!" the voice told him. For some reason Danny obeyed.

Danny's truck company was assigned backup position, called Second Due, so the men took their time about pulling out. Yet on the way Danny again felt "different," oddly focused on the call. As the siren sounded, his heart raced, as if he were being sent on a specific appointment. Was it God? God had always taken care of him, and Danny prays often. But this intense concentration was unusual. By the time the truck pulled up, Danny had already jumped off.

The tenement *was* burning, with flames shooting through windows on the third floor. The First Due company was on the scene but having trouble opening the hydrant, so Danny raced up the stairs, clogged with firefighters and fleeing tenants, to his assigned position as Forcible Entry Man. "I figured the others would catch up with me in a minute," he says. But because of the initial confusion, his buddies had inadvertantly gone into the building next door. Although firefighters should always operate in pairs, Danny was completely alone on the fourth floor.

Rather than put out the fire, a Forcible Entry Man opens a building, starting on the floor above the blaze, and searches for victims. It's a very precarious position, because smoke, heat, and flames go *up*. But when Danny got to the apartment and opened the steel fire door, he found something unusual. "I was surprised at the lack of smoke," he says, "considering the apartment below was fully involved." Carrying his tools, he crawled into the living room, keeping contact with the wall as a guide. No one was there. Then he worked his way toward the rear bedrooms.

At this point, the fire door on the third floor was opened, and heat and smoke came up the interior stairs and poured into the apartment. Danny inched his way down the hall to the first bedroom. Victims often become trapped in these buildings, but no one seemed to be here.

By now, the apartment felt like the inside of a chimney. Perspiration ran down Danny's face and neck, stinging his eyes. The intense heat reminded him that flames were getting closer, racing up the inside walls. Where were his buddies? Belatedly Danny realized that it was time to get out, before the floor collapsed. Strange, though. . . . He still had that sense of heightened awareness, of breath held, of something waiting to happen. Was God trying to reach him?

And then he heard it, just as he turned back. A tiny sound, coming from the second bedroom. A cough. A *baby's* cough.

No! Could anyone so small have survived in this temperature? Danny moved toward the sound, feeling his way into the other bedroom, and saw the hazy outline of a crib in the corner. Inside was a newborn infant.

The building residents let out a cheer when Danny staggered out the front door with the ten-day-old baby wrapped in his coat. "We were praying for you—and for him," one woman said before she took little Joel to the hospital.

The baby spent weeks in Intensive Care, but recovered completely. A neighbor had been watching him, but left in panic when the fire started. "I tried to tell Joel's family in the hospital that I think God has big plans for him, because if things didn't happen exactly as they did, he would not be here today," says Danny. "I'm not sure they understood."

But Danny understands—why he *had* to work that day, why he suited up completely for an expected false alarm, why he seemed propelled onto the fourth floor and strangely reluctant to leave. . . .

There are still dark moments in his life. But then he remembers the day God sent him on a heavenly mission—and the shadows flee.

A Sign for
Our Times

Knowing God's own time is best,
In patient hope I rest . . .

JOHN GREENLEAF WHITTIER

One morning in 1975 in Greenwood, South Carolina, Dorothy Nicholas sat scribbling at her kitchen table. She was trying to compose an appropriate slogan. Even though Dorothy is an award-winning writer and former advertising copywriter, she sometimes has trouble finding just the right words. And she sensed that these needed to be perfect.

The words were for a sign hanging over the self-service gas station Dorothy managed with help from her disabled husband, Fred. They had started working a week ago, pulling their trailer from Orlando up to Greenwood, and the job seemed simple enough, just sitting at a drive-up window, taking money from customers.

"It was a bit of a lark," Dorothy admits. "Fred and I called a lot of places 'home' during those years, because we both yearned to travel, and with our children grown, we could do it." Sometimes they settled for a while and took jobs, and this was one of those times.

There was already a lighted advertising sign on top of the building, but Dorothy's new boss had told her she could replace the message with anything she liked. "I had heard that this chain of stations was frequently robbed," Dorothy says, "so I was thinking about a safety-related slogan." At the same time, she felt that God was nudging her, encouraging her to make her trust in Him known to others. She tried several ideas, then inspiration struck.

"What do you think of this?" she asked Fred.

He studied her scrawl: *God Is Our Security Guard—-Always on the Job.* "That says it pretty well," he told her. The next day, he spelled it out on the lighted board.

The sign was impressive, but it seemed to have little or no effect on anyone. Few customers commented on it.

After five months, the wanderlust struck again, and Dorothy and Fred resigned and took off in the trailer. Time passed. "Sometimes we would travel that route, going from Florida to North Carolina, and I always felt a little glow as we'd drive by the sign," Dorothy says. Subsequent managers had liked it well enough to keep it up. But, remembering her strange urgency to find just the right words, Dorothy wondered if the sign had really mattered to God, after all.

In 1988, Dorothy and Fred found themselves in Gainesville, Florida. At church they met Janet* and Larry,* a young couple living nearby. The four got along well, and when Dorothy and Fred had some temporary health problems, their new friends proved to be a blessing, running errands, providing an occasional meal, and just being there. "I don't know what we would have done without you," Dorothy told Larry more than once. She was growing quite fond of this kind, clean-cut young man.

One evening Dorothy invited Janet and Larry over for dinner. The four sat around the table, talking leisurely. Fred and Dorothy were surprised to hear that Larry had grown up in Greenwood.

"Why, we worked there once—" Dorothy began. Had they ever met Larry? She started to ask him, but having begun to talk about himself, Larry couldn't stop.

"I've had a pretty rough past," he went on, pent-up words suddenly tumbling out. At sixteen, he'd gotten involved with the wrong crowd and had spent a year in reform school. After his release, he'd wanted to start over again, but because of his record, he couldn't find a job.

"One night in 1975," Larry continued, "I decided to rob a gas station for money to leave home." There was a self-service station nearby, so he stole his father's gun and car, and just before closing time, he drove up to rob the woman sitting at the window.

But before pulling his gun, he glanced at the roof of the building. There had always been a sign there, but someone had recently changed the words. "When I read that message," Larry said, "I knew I couldn't rob that place—or do anything else illegal." He went home, prayed all night and begged God to help him straighten out his life.

Dorothy and Fred looked at each other. "What did the sign say, Larry?" she asked gently.

"I've never forgotten those words," the young man assured her. "It said, 'God Is Our Security Guard—Always on the Job.' And He is, Dorothy. He guarded me from danger that night, and He has ever since."

Dorothy's heart lifted. It had taken thirteen years, but now she knew the source of that strange longing, the need to find just the perfect words. For God had used her small act of faith to bring a lost child safely to His side.

A Light unto
Her Path

The world is charged with the grandeur of God,
It will flame out like shining from shook foil.

GERALD MANLEY HOPKINS, *"GOD'S GRANDEUR"*

$\mathcal{M}$argaret Baucom of Shreveport, Louisiana, a private-duty nurse, had been caring for an elderly man for several nights in a row. Usually her shift ended about seven, but the man's wife had awakened early one morning and told Margaret to go home and get some much-needed sleep. Margaret pulled away from the house in somewhat of a fog, so tired that she forgot to press her automatic door lock. She would avoid the high-speed interstate, she decided, yawning, and take a slower route home. "It went through a tough section of town, but I assumed no one would be up at four A.M.," she says.

Margaret was wrong. Drowsily, she drove down the seedy, poorly lit avenue, then stopped for a traffic light behind the only other car in view. Almost immediately, all four doors opened, and Margaret saw three young men get out of the three passenger seats. Slowly they started toward her, menacing, terrifying.

Margaret's heart started to pound. Her doors were unlocked! And for the life of her, she couldn't remember where the automatic switch was!

Everything seemed to click into slow motion, "as if a record or movie had been slowed down," Margaret says. Wildly she considered putting the car in reverse or speeding up to run over them. But she seemed paralyzed with fear. "God, help me. . . ." It was all Margaret could think to murmur.

Instantly two enormous headlights shone right behind her, as if a huge eighteen-wheeler had pulled up inches from her rear bumper. The lights beamed through her car and seemed to flood the entire avenue with a radiant white glow. Margaret looked at the storefronts, the parking lot several yards ahead . . . everything was bathed in brilliance. "It was brighter than the pictures on television of the Gulf War bombing raids," she says.

Yet how could that be? For she had heard no truck approaching, no sound of an engine revving or shifting gears. And despite the powerful glare behind her, the night was completely hushed.

At that moment the driver emerged from the car in front of Margaret and started toward her too. *Oh, God, please!* she prayed. She was going to die here. She knew it. Then, incredibly, Margaret saw a look of shock, fear, *terror* replace the young man's threatening expression. "He put his hands way up, almost in a gesture of apology toward the light," Margaret says, "and backed up right into the car." The others jumped in, and the car sped off and squealed around the next corner.

Margaret slumped against the seat, almost weeping in relief. It had all happened so fast! Had it been a dream? But, no, the headlights were still there. Slowly she stepped on the gas and pulled away from the corner.

The twin beacons followed her, illuminating the night in a glow that was almost . . . heavenly. Margaret began to feel serene, protected, almost blessed. And yet there wasn't a sound behind her.

When she reached a forested area, she saw the lights silently turn off to the left and disappear. Just a few blocks more and she was safely home. "I was shaking, almost a holy trembling, and my husband knew something important had happened," Margaret remembers. She told him of her close call.

"Where did you say the truck turned off?" Bob asked.

"Right at the woods." Margaret described the scene. Bob shook his head. "It did, Bob," she insisted. "I saw it go left."

There was a look of wonder on Bob's face. "Margaret, nothing could turn there. There's no road anywhere near the woods."

Margaret still wonders what the driver of the car saw behind her that night. But she'll never forget the silent, steadfast beacons that came as a "light unto her path."

Mysterious Medication

[Miracles are] momentary glimpses into a mystery of such power, depth and beauty that if we were to see it head on . . . we would be annihilated.

FREDERICK BUECHNER, *SPIRITUAL QUESTS*

*J*anuary 20, 1992, in Larsen, Wisconsin, dawned sunny but bitterly cold. A good day to stay inside, Mary Mueller decided, hoping that her pager would remain mute. In addition to working a factory swing shift and running a 131-acre farm, Mary is a member of the Clayton-Winchester Township volunteer fire department, and she relishes her downtime.

In the middle of a shower and shampoo, however, Mary heard the pager squawking details about a car on fire less than two miles away. The dispatcher requested not only fire trucks, but also the Jaws of Life. It sounded serious.

Although Mary's adrenaline always races at a call, this time she felt literally propelled. She barely dried herself, stuffed her dripping hair under a helmet, raced into the subzero morning, and leaped into her pickup. Because this was a daytime call at the far end of the district's rural boundary, Mary knew that farmers would be the only ones responding—and that could take a long time.

Except for the passing volunteer who had phoned in the report, Mary was the first rescue worker on the scene. It resembled the aftermath of an explosion. Although there was no fire (first accounts were inaccurate), a pile of twisted metal lay on the highway. Wreckage was strewn across the fields and road shoulder. To Mary, the site seemed mysteriously stripped of color, ominous in black, white, and gray.

There was no sign of a second vehicle. Mary would later learn that a semitrailer had been pulling a front-end loader with metal tracks, on a flatbed. An oncoming compact car carrying three University of Wisconsin students had swerved into the protruding steel treads, which had sheared off the car's roof like a giant can opener. The truckdriver had continued on for another mile or so, initially unaware of the accident.

But now Mary investigated quickly. A young man, obviously dead, lay under the station wagon's left front bumper. The other volunteer was consoling a young woman pinned inside the wreckage. Mary rounded the metal tangle toward the passenger side, then stopped. Was that a third body in the ditch? She ran, sliding down the incline on her knees.

A blond girl, about twenty-one, looked up at Mary with terrified eyes. Mary felt an instant bond. "I'm Mary," she told the young woman. "I'm a firefighter, and we're going to help you, but we need your cooperation, okay?"

The girl nodded, trembling. "I'm Lori."

Before moving a patient, rescue workers must make an assessment. Gently, Mary examined Lori's left side and found only a bruised calf. "When I got to her right shoulder, it literally fell out into my hand," Mary says. "I padded it up the best I could, and kept looking."

But as she lifted a lock of Lori's hair to check a trickle of blood, Mary gasped. She was looking at a gash at least six inches long and three inches wide, forming a pool of blood underneath the girl. Lori's heavy clothes and matted hair had hidden the horrible fact that she was bleeding to death right in front of Mary.

How could she stop the flow? Mary had first-aid and CPR training, "but firefighters are primarily expected to fight fires," she notes. "We don't carry medical supplies—everything is on the equipment van." Coming from miles away, the van might not arrive for fifteen or twenty minutes. Mary needed pressure bandages immediately. What about her fireman's gloves? No. They were big enough but dirty, and pressing them against such a terrible wound would introduce more infection. "God," Mary prayed, "please help me help her. There's no way I can do this on my own."

What could she use? Worried, Mary looked to her left. Nothing but fresh, undisturbed snow across the fields. She glanced to her right, to a group of bystanders forming along the highway. Maybe one of them had something sterile to stem the flow. For a moment, she looked back at Lori—and her heart seemed to stop. In the snow to Mary's left, half an arm's length away, "just where you want your material," sat a dark-red bag with black handles and a black medical emblem.

Who had brought it in that split second when Mary had looked away? There was no one near her, no footprints marring the smooth snow. And the bag looked nothing like the fluorescent-orange ones local EMS personnel used.

Mary didn't have time to wonder. She hit the clip, and the bag snapped open to reveal a veritable pharmacy. Rubber gloves, tape, bandages, and absorbent squares of every kind and size, all sealed in sterile containers—everything that she needed was there, in the order in which she would need it. Quickly Mary went to work, applying as much pressure as she could against the gaping hole, adding new gauze squares as the old ones became saturated.

"Come to the hospital with me, Mary, please," Lori murmured.

"I will, honey. Just hang on."

Firefighters didn't go to hospitals with victims as a rule, but Mary couldn't imagine leaving this girl. Something seemed to be holding them together in a protective glass bubble, shielded from the horror, somehow safe. Mary knew the Life Flight helicopter had arrived—she could hear the engine descending. But she and Lori didn't feel the propeller's blast of wind. Nor was either of them cold, despite the subzero temperatures.

As personnel loaded the other girl into the helicopter, paramedics arrived and ran to assess Lori's condition. "Stay with me, Mary," Lori pleaded, her voice fading now.

Mary nodded. Her fingers ached with the strain, and her hair had frozen solid under her helmet. But she still felt that strange—and loving—connection. They would have to pry her away from Lori.

But Lori had lost too much blood to survive a helicopter trip. "There's only one thing to do, Mary," a paramedic decided. "You're going to hold Lori's life in your hands—literally."

"How?"

"We'll show you." Quickly, the paramedics taped Mary's hands against Lori's wound, and then to the backboard. It took six men to haul both women out of the ditch without disturbing their arrangement. Sirens screamed, lights flashed.

Mary smiled down at the girl as the van raced against time. "I told you we'd stay together," she reminded her.

It was hours before both victims stabilized and Mary felt able to relinquish her link with Lori. Only then did she remember the mysterious medical bag. She drove back to the scene to retrieve it.

Several firefighters had seen Mary using the bag and had assumed it was hers. If anyone had come across it, he would have returned it to her. Nor had the site been left unattended. Since the accident, it had been under constant surveillance. The medical bag, however, had mysteriously vanished. And although workers painstakingly collected all accident fragments, no trace of discarded bandages, wrappings, gauze, or other debris from the bag was ever found.

Today, Mary and Lori enjoy a close friendship, forged during those desperate moments in a ditch, when both felt held in the Divine Physician's hands.

Rescues
on the Road

May the road rise up to meet you,
May the wind be always at your back . . .
And may God hold you in the palm of His hand.

IRISH BLESSING

*M*iracles happen frequently as we drive. Barbara Brownell
still marvels at the memory of visiting her pregnant daughter-
in-law in Palmer, Alaska. Marce was due any minute and could
not wedge herself behind her van's steering wheel. So Barbara,
although nervous about the unfamiliar terrain, volunteered to
drive them on a shopping trip.

The road was winding, with dense forest right up to the pavement. They passed a sign: *Caution—Narrow Bridge Ahead.*

What if a car is coming from the other direction? Barbara
worried silently. There would be no place for either vehicle to
pull off.

Zipping around the curve, Barbara found herself almost upon
the bridge—with her fear confirmed. She heard Marce gasp. A
semitruck was speeding toward them. They would meet in the

middle of the bridge! But even two compact cars wouldn't have enough room to pass.

Barbara thought of Marce, the new baby, the trauma for her son. . . . She closed her eyes tightly. "Please, God, not now," she whispered, then aimed straight ahead.

A few seconds passed. Barbara opened her eyes. They had crossed safely and were on the other side of the bridge. Neither could see the truck anywhere.

Ardith Muse and her husband had separated, but were now reunited and trying to make their stormy marriage work. However, Ardith could not forget Bob, a man she had met during the separation. Although Bob lived in another city, four driving hours away, Ardith felt irresistibly drawn to him.

One night Ardith and her husband had an argument, and Ardith stomped out of the house. She would go to Bob, she decided. On the expressway, however, she had second thoughts. Hadn't she promised her husband not to see Bob anymore? Wasn't she committed to work on her marriage? Of what value was her word, her vow, if she could break it in a fit of temper?

Four hours later, as she pulled up in front of Bob's apartment, Ardith had made her decision. She turned around and started back. If she hurried, maybe she could reach home before her husband left for work.

"About five-thirty A.M., with an hour's driving time left, I noticed there were no cars around me, just a cluster about a quarter mile back," she says. "So I took the opportunity to open my seat belt and stretch my back." At that moment her car hit a puddle of spilled diesel fuel, invisible in the dark, and went into a wild spin.

"I grew up in Michigan, so I know how to come out of a slide," Ardith says. But none of the techniques worked. Her car kept revolving at sixty miles per hour, and Ardith had no seat belt on! How soon would the cars behind her catch up and crash into her? Ardith pictured herself dead, her husband never knowing that she had been coming back to him.

"Long ago I had walked away from Jesus," Ardith says. "But I always knew He loved me anyway. Now, I took my hands off the steering wheel and said, 'God, You're in control.' " She shut her eyes, waiting for the impact.

But nothing happened. Seconds passed, the car stopped, and Ardith peeked. Her car was off the road, behind a guardrail, purring quietly, yet in Drive gear. Ardith jumped out. What had happened to the cars behind her? She looked back—and gasped.

They were still a quarter mile behind her! Although several minutes had surely passed, the approaching vehicles had seemingly covered no distance during that time. Ardith knelt on the wet grass, tears spilling down her cheeks. "Thank you, God. Thank you!" was all she could say.

Ardith didn't see her husband that morning. But she recommitted herself to Jesus and asked Him to restore her marriage. Today, five years later, the couple have two children, and a wonderful relationship, built on faith—and the memory of a night when God made time stand still.

Maureen M. left a party later than she had intended, with a passenger to take home. "It was a miserable night, dark and drizzly, with fog rolling in," she says.

She let off her companion about two-thirty A.M., with ten miles still ahead of her. But by now, the fog had thickened and she could hardly see. "The route was all wooded, with streams alongside the road and many narrow turns," Maureen recalls. "Visibility was so poor that I tried holding my car door open, looking down at the road's white line as a marker."

What should she do? There were few if any houses along the route. Besides, would she ring a stranger's doorbell at this late hour? Going back to her friend's house would be just as risky as driving on to her own. Would she be safe—or warm enough—if she parked?

She kept driving, but the haze thickened. Suddenly the radio stopped. With a sinking heart, Maureen realized that her battery must be dying. The car lights flickered, dimmed—then went out. Maureen often prays when she drives, but this time she *pleaded*. "Holy Spirit, this is one for You," she murmured. "I can't see anything at all. You'll have to drive this car for me."

Miles passed. Maureen continued to drive slowly, although she had no lights. She clung to the steering wheel as if it were a lifeline, and, occasionally, for no apparent reason, she turned right or left, somehow staying on the pavement. Nothing passed her, and she could see no outline of the road, no tree shapes or road signs—fog enfolded the car to within an inch in all directions. It was like driving in gray cotton candy. Would this terrible journey ever end?

Finally, the engine coughed, chugged, and slowed. The battery must be almost dead now. *God, take care of me . . .* Maureen prayed.

The car rolled to a gentle, final stop. At least it hadn't careened down an embankment. But where was she? Hesitantly, Maureen opened the door and got out, shuffling alongside the car, her hands out in front of her to brace a fall.

Wait! There was a shape just ahead, about a foot from the car's front bumper. It looked like the outline of a building. But how. . . ? Maureen went a step or two farther, right up to it. She looked, looked again, then got on her knees in tearful gratitude.

She was in her driveway.

*   *   *

That wasn't the only miracle in Maureen's life. Her father, Hugh*, was touched by one too:

When Hugh bought his pickup truck, he put a little cross in the glove compartment as a bit of added travel protection. Then he closed the compartment and promptly forgot about it.

One day when Hugh was driving through a large city on a congested highway, a driver lost control of his car and slammed into Hugh's truck. Witnesses told Hugh later that he was thrown through the open passenger-side window on impact. The pickup flipped over and over again, landing on its roof and narrowly missing other cars.

Hugh was temporarily unconscious, but he soon awakened and, unaware of the seriousness of the crash, got to his feet. People ran toward him. "Lie down, lie down!" they shouted. "You must be hurt!"

"Not at all." Hugh felt just fine. But he looked at his upside-down pickup some yards away in wonder. How had he survived without injuries?

His head was clearing, and as the sound of an emergency vehicle drew near, Hugh realized there was something in his right hand. He looked down. He was holding his little cross.

It was the night that the Chicago Bears won the Super Bowl. Michele Malec celebrated by taking drugs—and overdosing. "I awakened on my hallway floor, having trouble breathing," she says. "When I went to take a Valium and looked in the mirror, my face was bluish-gray."

Michele was scared. "God, please help me," she prayed. She got to her car, sat behind the wheel, but doesn't recall starting the car or opening the garage door. There seemed to be a bright light shining in front of her. Then she awakened in Little

Company of Mary Hospital's emergency room, surrounded by medical personnel.

Everyone's face was blurry, except one man's. "He was about thirty, very calm and kind," she says. "He spoke gently to me, as if he loved me, and I felt peaceful." Michele fell asleep again.

On Michele's third day as a patient, a man poked his head into her room. "Just stopped by to see how you were doing," he told her.

"Do I know you?" Michele asked.

"I'm the security guard in the emergency room," the man told her. "I was on duty the night you came in."

"I don't remember that," Michele admitted ruefully. "How did I get here? Did you see who brought me in?"

The guard hesitated. "No one brought you," he said finally. "But. . . ."

"I saw your car come into the parking lot," the guard explained slowly. "You were slumped over the wheel, unconscious. When the car pulled up, I opened your door. Nobody was inside but you."

But that was impossible. How could she have driven an unfamiliar three-mile journey over snowy streets while unconscious—and not have crashed?

A few weeks later, Michelle went to the hospital for a checkup. "That young doctor in the emergency room," she asked. "Who was he?"

"There was no young doctor there," her physician answered. "There were just my partner and me—and we were busy because your heart stopped on the examining table."

"It did!"

"You're a lucky young woman," he went on. "Someone must be looking out for you."

Michele thought of her dangerous drive, her brush with death, the Man with the warm eyes and the loving smile. "Someone is," she said.

Michele's life is much richer now. Each day she places all her problems in God's hands.

Book Two

ANGEL
MIRACLES

Angels in Our Midst

Wouldn't it be wonderful if, as you read these words, an angel whispers in your ear, speaking of God's unconditional love for you, words you can hear if you listen carefully?

MITCH FINLEY, *EVERYBODY HAS A GUARDIAN ANGEL*

When Randy Owen left his office to do some errands on a drizzly day, his mother, Nathalie, was concerned. Ice storms are common in Dallas, and her worry increased as the temperature plummeted. "Angels," she said, "please put a ring of protection around Randy, wherever he drives today."

Randy returned, and Nathalie hugged him in relief. "Mom," he said excitedly, "you'll never believe this!" At an overpass, about a dozen cars had lost control at the same time, including his. They slid, spun, and eventually stopped. "Everything seemed to happen in slow motion," Randy explained. "But though we ended up facing every which way, we were all about an inch apart—and no one was hit!" The drivers had gotten out and examined one another's cars in amazement. How could such a thing have happened?

Nathalie just smiled—and sent thanksgiving heavenward.

*　　*　　*

Karen Sue and Mike Reilly went with some young missionaries to Amsterdam, The Netherlands, to witness about Jesus. Karen Sue had never done anything like this before, and she felt awkward and shy.

One day the young people marched into a dangerous section of the city. More experienced members warned the novices that the people living there would harass and throw things at them. As they went along, singing and praising God, Karen Sue became very nervous.

Then, as she looked over her right shoulder, she spotted a blond man in light clothing. He was walking a shiny ten-speed bike, and he was smiling at her. "There was a glow about him," she recalls. "And it was strange, because most people in Amsterdam wear dark clothes. And no one has such a bike—they are all rusty with fat tires—and his would have been stolen the first time he parked it in that area."

Somehow, Karen Sue had become the last one marching. But now she didn't feel anxious at all. Occasionally, she looked over her shoulder to see the man following her, watching her. Would she get a chance to talk with him?

The walk ended safely in front of the mission's coffee shop. But Karen Sue's escort had disappeared. She understood. He had guarded her through the dark part of her journey, and there was no need for her to see him anymore.

George sat next to me on a plane, and he told of a time when he had moved to a new city and was living alone, unconnected to friends or family. "I most remember the intense loneliness," he said. At times it was so painful that he wondered if life was even worth the struggle.

One evening he entered a restaurant for a solitary meal. The smiling host approached him. "Table for two?" he asked.

What was wrong with the man? George wondered. "For *one*," he answered firmly.

The host looked puzzled, and he escorted George to a table for two, where he pulled out both chairs.

Soon a waitress approached. She set down two menus and poured two glasses of ice water. Preoccupied, George barely noticed.

But when his dinner came, something began to happen. As if on a mental scroll, George began to *see* his blessings. He had health, eyesight, a decent job, a nice apartment . . . most of all, God loved him. George hadn't thought about God for a while. He had been trying to handle everything himself. Now, as he ate, he could almost feel his depression lifting, being replaced by cheerful anticipation. Life wasn't so bad, after all.

By the time George approached the counter with his check, he was smiling. The cashier smiled back as she handed him his change. "Guess your friend wasn't hungry tonight, hmm?" she commented.

George was almost to his car before it finally sank in. Three restaurant employees had apparently seen someone with him that evening. Was it an elaborate hoax? If so, how could anyone account for the unexpected feeling of well-being that now permeated his spirit after months of misery?

"I think my angel came to bring me faith and comfort, in a way that would leave no doubt," George told me. "It was a turning point for me."

Whether we can see angels or not, whether they come as ordinary-looking people or as apparitions, they are indeed evidence of miraculous intervention, answers to prayer. Angels act as liaisons between heaven and earth (the word *angel* comes from a Greek word meaning *messenger*), and also protect us from harm. Of course, God often touches us directly. But angels are mentioned more than three hundred times in Scripture, so God obviously intended them to play an important part in His plan.

The idea of angels is prevalent in Judaism, Christianity, and Islam. But interest in them declined in the eighteenth century during the Age of Enlightenment, with its emphasis on reason and science. When the Reverend Billy Graham decided to preach on angels in the early 1970s, he found little or nothing had been written about them for decades. Graham not only undertook a study on the subject, but he also wrote *Angels: God's Secret Agents*, which became a best-seller and probably the forerunner of our current angel revival. "In the midst of the world crisis through which we are destined to live in the years ahead," he wrote, "the subject of angels will be of great comfort and inspiration to believers in God—and a challenge to unbelievers to believe."

He was right. Today, people are reading up on angels, asking their guardian angel to intercede for them or a loved one—and examining the "coincidences" in their own lives with growing awareness. A December 1993 *Time*/CNN poll reported that 69% of Americans believe angels exist. An earlier Gallup poll found that 75% of teenagers believe in angels. Angels are also providing reassurance in the midst of confusion. "I cannot tell you how wonderful I feel, knowing that I have a spiritual companion," one former skeptic wrote to me.

According to their intrigued parents, an increasing number of young children seem to be seeing angels too. "Our preschooler seemed so surprised when I told him I could not see the angel in his room," a father wrote. On another occasion, after a hysterical mother had suddenly calmed down and successfully performed CPR on her unconscious baby, her three-year-old asked, "Mommy, who was that man behind you with his hand on your shoulder?" The mother hadn't seen or felt anyone nearby.[3]

Perhaps to children, heaven is still a faint but specific memory, and they remain easily connected to both worlds for a while. We should remain open to these experiences, for our little ones may have much to teach us.

It's important to remember that while angels weave in and out of history—and our lives—they are never a stand-in for God. They intercede at His call, carry His concern and love to us, bring us His miraculous peace that passes all understanding. "Angels belong to a uniquely different dimension of creation that we, limited to the natural order, can scarcely comprehend," says the Reverend Graham.

But when one touches us, we know it. . . .

Miracle at
Christmas

This is what you are to hold fast to yourself—the
sympathy and companionship of the unseen worlds.

PHILLIPS BROOKS, EPISCOPAL BISHOP

In 1955, Emilie Long's husband, a career Army officer, left active duty and found a consulting job that involved traveling about twenty days each month. Emilie and their three school-age children moved to a hilltop dwelling in New England where Emilie's parents lived. "They were elderly and needed as much care as the children," Emilie says. It was a busy time for her.

Emilie had enjoyed being a military wife, but she was looking forward to settling down. Her only regret was that there would be no additions to the Long family. Several years earlier, she had had surgery that would probably prevent another pregnancy. Emilie prayed the doctors were wrong, but she was almost forty, and the possibility of a miracle grew fainter each year.

Emilie hadn't been settled long when she came down with a fierce virus. It sidelined her for weeks, but when she went to her doctor for a final checkup, she noticed that instead of losing weight during her ordeal, she had actually gained. "The doctor thought I had a tumor," she recalls, "but when he sent me for tests, neither of us could believe it." Emilie was going to have a baby.

In the midst of her joy, however, there was apprehension. No normal delivery was possible, the doctor said. Emilie, already high-risk because of her age, must go to a specialist in another city for a cesarean section. The due date was debatable. December? January? In the 1950s, technology couldn't be more specific. And was the baby healthy, or had the virus affected it?

With her husband away much of the time, and several people depending on her, Emilie wondered how she would manage.

Fall turned into winter. Emilie did chores, talked to her husband long-distance, watched over her parents and her children, and prayed for God's protection for her unborn baby. But there were times, especially when the house quieted at night and she contemplated the difficult path ahead, when her faith wavered— just a bit.

Christmas vacation from school was about to begin the day Emilie left for an assessment from the specialist. "He was going to do a final X ray, which should show when the baby would be large enough to deliver," she says. It was cold, and snow had started to fall, but the twenty-mile drive through picturesque New England towns was uneventful. However, Emilie walked out of the doctor's office right into a blizzard.

Her first thought was of her children. Her parents could care for them only so long without needing help themselves. The sooner she reached home, the better. But the roads were treacherous now. What about her own safety and the baby's? What if she crashed or slid into a ditch? Would anyone find her?

Once again, she felt that terrible isolation. If only she wasn't so alone!

The journey seemed to take hours. Emilie prayed nonstop, her muscles aching as she struggled to keep the car on the road and to see through the whirling flakes. There was little traffic, but as she approached the last mile, she realized the incline was too slippery. She turned toward a longer, but less steep back route.

Carefully Emilie maneuvered up the back road, slow enough to keep traction (and to stop if any cars approached), but fast enough to prevent skidding or getting stuck. There was one right turn to make, then the final slope. The snow was icing, thick under her wheels. Emilie turned, increased speed, spun out, and stalled.

Oh, dear God. . . . She was stuck now, with visibility almost nil and a steep hill in front of her. Perhaps she could climb it on foot. But the abandoned car would be a hazard to any unsuspecting motorist. There was sand in the trunk. Should she try to spread it or to dig herself out? Emilie thought of the shovel and the strain digging would put on her already-exhausted body. But what else could she do?

Leaving the engine idling, she opened the door, then stopped in surprise. A tall man was making his way across the road toward her. He wore a long, dark-gray overcoat, and his hat was pulled over his eyes against the blowing snow. A station wagon stood just behind him, facing her. It was strange that she hadn't seen or heard it until now.

"Stay in the car!" the man called to Emilie. "I'll get you out!" His voice brooked no argument, and Emilie did as she was told.

The man went behind her car, and in a minute, she felt it begin to move, climbing the hill easily through the deepening drifts. How incredibly strong he was, Emilie thought, to push the car so quickly. She couldn't see him in her rearview mirror, but when she had reached the top, she braked, opened the window, and leaned out to shout her thanks.

But she saw no station wagon. Nor was a helpful figure standing behind her, waving her on. Emilie's bewildered gaze fell on the snowy road next to her car. Soon the plows would clear a path for the evening commuters. But now, not a track or footprint marred the white blanket, even though the station wagon must have driven *toward* her, past this very spot.

The real Christmas arrived for the Longs when baby Peter did, just a few weeks after December 25. And as Emilie held her small miracle in her arms, she gave silent thanks. She had thought she was alone, but she knew better now. Like another mother from a long-ago time, she had gone through a perilous journey and placed her trust in God. And He had sent angels to guard her in all her ways.

Protector in the Barn

. . . [I]f angels fight,
Weak men must fall, for heaven still guards
the right.

SHAKESPEARE, *RICHARD II*

$\mathcal{E}$ver since fifth grade, Katie Lowell* and Michelle Sanders* had ridden horses together in the rural East Coast area where they both live. By the time Katie turned thirteen in 1980, she was the proud owner of Blaze, a beautiful chestnut with white markings on his face. Since Michelle lived on a huge farm with lots of barns and pastures, Katie boarded Blaze there. "Every morning before school, my dad dropped me at the barn door on his way to work," Katie explains. "I fed Blaze and turned him out on one of the pastures. Then Michelle and I walked down a long driveway to meet the school bus."

After school, the girls retraced their steps, walking from the bus stop back to the farm. "Sometimes I wouldn't see Blaze because of the rolling hills," Katie says. "But I'd call him, and he'd gallop in, full speed." The girls would brush their horses and saddle up so they could ride a bit before dark. Eventually

Katie's father would arrive to take his daughter home. It was a perfect arrangement.

Usually Michelle went home before Katie's father arrived. Since the other horse boarders weren't around at that time, Katie was alone. "But I loved it," she says. "The farm was a peaceful place, and I was never afraid."

One pleasant afternoon in late October, Katie and Michelle jumped off the school bus and ran up the driveway to the pasture where their horses waited. The girls rode for a while, and eventually the shadows lengthened.

"Have to help with dinner," Michelle sighed, slipping off her horse and turning him out to the pasture. Michelle always had kitchen chores to do.

Katie opened her mouth to say good-bye to her friend, then stopped. She felt odd. In fact, for no apparent reason, she was suddenly afraid. "Do you *have* to go?" she asked.

Michelle shot her a puzzled look. "Well, sure. I never get to stay out as late as you, you know that."

"Can't you ride just a little longer?" Katie heard herself plead. Her strange apprehension was growing by the minute.

Michelle looked even more perplexed. "Of course not. And, anyway, it's getting dark and your dad will be here soon. See you tomorrow!" With a wave, she headed toward her house.

Katie didn't wave back. By now she was extremely frightened. Yet everything seemed normal. Why this strange agitation? She would finish her barn chores quickly and wait outside for her father, she decided. Usually, it was hard to leave the farm, but tonight she longed to see his car.

Katie led Blaze into his stall and hurriedly brushed him down. Being inside the barn made her even more nervous, as if she were being watched. Yet, no one was there. Finally, she finished. But just before leaving, she realized that the horses were short of hay. She'd need to go up into the loft and throw some down.

"The barn's top three floors were used to store hay," Katie says. "The floor above the stalls was divided into four corners, one for each horse, so we boarders would know how much hay we were using and when we needed to buy more."

Katie climbed the hayloft ladder under her corner. With each step, her feeling of dread increased. Something was terribly wrong. She knew it, without knowing *how* she knew it. Instinct told her to run, that she was in danger, that something terrible was going to happen. But it was unthinkable that her beloved Blaze should be left without hay. At the top of the ladder, she put her hand on the door and started to push.

"Katie," a voice said over her left shoulder. "Katie, close the door. Do not go up there. Go out, sit quietly, and wait for your father."

The voice was not loud. Nor was it either male or female, "but it felt masculine," Katie says. It was calm, firm, precise— and not at all frightening. But it *commanded*.

Startled, Katie turned in the direction of the voice. But no one was behind her. There was no one at all in the barn.

She didn't hesitate. Quickly climbing down the ladder, Katie scooted out and waited in the usual place for her father. As soon as he came, she jumped into the car. "I didn't feel safe," she says, "until the barn was completely out of sight."

The next morning before school, Katie's father drove her to the farm. But as they reached the barn, they saw police cars surrounding it.

Katie's father got out of the car. "What's going on?" he asked an officer.

Katie followed him, worried. Was Blaze all right? What had happened?

"Everything's okay now," the police officer reassured them. "But yesterday, a violent inmate escaped from a mental hospital and wound up here."

"Here?" Katie's heart started to pound.

"Yeah." The policeman pointed to the side of the barn near Blaze's stall. "He was hiding up in the loft, on a bed of hay he'd made on this corner."

Her corner. Where her hay was kept. Where she had almost opened the loft door. . . .

The officer shook his head. "He had a three-pronged pitchfork lying beside him, in case someone got in his way. Lucky no one did—until we caught him just now."

Lucky? Katie remembered the unnamed terror that had surrounded her, the loving voice that had sent her out of the barn to safety, and knew—would always know—that it was far more than that.

Hospital Helpers

*One should not stand at the foot of a sick person's bed,
because that place is reserved for the guardian angel.*

JEWISH FOLK SAYING

Carole Mott-McCay was working the evening shift at a New England nursing home when one of the most difficult patients rang for assistance. "He was a proud man from the old country, angry about his placement in the home, and sometimes nasty with the staff," Carole says. "But when I came to him that night, he was serene and pleasant."

The man told Carole he was cold and asked for his favorite yellow sweater. As she went to the closet, she heard him say very softly, "You're so beautiful. You look just like an angel. . . ."

Carole turned, the sweater in her hands, and realized the man had peacefully died. Was he talking to Carole? "No," she says. "I am certain he saw something I didn't."

Ten days after Virginia Lee of Wauchula, Florida, had her first baby, the infant contracted meningitis, which left her profoundly brain damaged. "My prayer changed from 'God, heal Brenda' to 'Father, since I am unable to reach into Brenda's world, please be with her. Let Your angels entertain her and show her the love I can't,' " says Virginia.

The following years were difficult. Virginia met parents of handicapped children who were bitter and bereaved, but, somehow, she was able to love Brenda wholeheartedly. The hardest part was not being able to penetrate her daughter's "veil."

"Due to the severe damage to her nervous system, Brenda cried constantly, and I was at a loss as to how to comfort her," Virginia says. Yet sometimes the crying would stop abruptly, and Virginia would rush in, to find Brenda lying quietly, an enchanted expression on her face, as if she were daydreaming. At times, she would even smile.

During these moments Virginia felt certain that someone was lovingly ministering to her daughter, that Brenda had "inside information" about heaven. But Virginia never knew for sure.

Brenda died in a residential home when she was twenty-five. As Virginia sat waiting for the doctor, a caregiver from the home came to Virginia. "I have something to tell you," she began hesitantly.

Shortly before Brenda died, the caregiver had been going down the hall. As she reached the end, she turned and saw a dark-haired woman in a nurse's uniform walking toward Brenda's room. "I knew she wasn't part of the staff, so I called to her," the worker explained. "But she turned into Brenda's room without responding."

The caregiver had hurried to the room. But no one was with Brenda.

Virginia began to weep. "All I could think to tell the caregiver was that she had witnessed the answer to my twenty-five-year prayer," Virginia says. Brenda had, indeed, been in touch with the angels, and one had come to take her safely home.

*　　*　　*

Stories abound about angels escorting us to heaven. But death is not the only time angels visit hospitals. Healing angels also seem to roam corridors, unseen except by a chosen few. Nurse and author Joy Snell reports often seeing such a being, "flitting among the patients, and here and there laying her hand on the forehead of some sufferer. Often, after such a treatment, has a patient said to me on awaking, 'Oh, nurse, I feel so much better this morning.' "[4]

Perhaps angels of mercy also disguise themselves as hospital staff members. In 1985, Lynda Butcavage underwent a difficult cancer operation at Nazareth Hospital in Philadelphia. In Intensive Care, she awoke to see a nurse near her bed, a plain young woman with gentle blue eyes and blond hair that was pulled back in a bun.

"I'm here to take care of you, Lynda." The nurse bent over and affectionately rubbed Lynda's cheek with the side of her hand. "You're going to be okay."

Everything hurt, and Lynda was frightened. But during the next few hours, the nurse stayed nearby, talking gently to her. "I sensed somehow that she was special, and a calmness seemed to cover me," Lynda says. The nurse didn't do any medical procedures for her, although others did. The woman was simply . . . there.

Eventually, the nurse stroked Lynda's cheek once more. "I must leave you now," she said softly. "But I promise you I will be with you again."

"When?" Lynda asked sleepily.

The nurse smiled. "Soon."

During the difficult days that followed, Lynda kept watching for her special nurse. But the woman didn't return. After she was discharged, Lynda and her husband went to the ICU to find the nurse. But the staff was at a loss. None of them had seen that woman with Lynda, and no one fitting her description worked on any ICU shift.

Lynda has had several surgeries since, but she has never again met her special angel. "Still, her loveliness has stayed with me and I can picture her vividly," Lynda says. "I hope that I will meet her—and hug her—in heaven."

Margaret phoned KDKA Radio in Pittsburgh to share her story. A victim of a heart attack, she was being transported by ambulance to a hospital, when she had a near-death experience. "I remember leaving my body and hovering above it—as others have described," she said. "I saw myself lying on the stretcher, with sirens screaming and people working over me, but I wasn't afraid. My body seemed like a thing, nothing to worry about. The feeling of peace was exquisite."

Margaret thought that she might float away from the scene. Then she noticed that, amid all the activity, there was a young man sitting on a bench alongside her body, looking at her intensely. "He was wearing a white shirt and pants, and an expression of deep concern," Margaret remembers. "He never took his eyes off me. I remember wondering why—with everyone else so busy—he was just sitting there."

A moment later, however, instead of drifting away, Margaret felt herself "slither" back into her body. The scene she was watching disappeared, and she later awakened in Intensive Care.

Margaret recovered, and later she called the ambulance service to ask if they could look at their records and tell her who the young man was. But the records showed no man in attendance during Margaret's journey. All the people involved in her care had been women. In addition, no man matching that description was employed by the ambulance service. And the uniforms the workers wore were not white.

"I've always heard that angels keep their eyes on us from the moment we are created until they deliver us to God," Margaret said. "I'm glad to know that mine is on the job."

Janis Reed agrees. She brought her three-week-old daughter to Schumpert Memorial Hospital in Shreveport, Louisiana, because of a serious stomach ailment. Technicians took the baby to be tested, and Janis went into the empty parents' waiting room and collapsed, weeping. Her baby was so young. What was wrong with her? What if they couldn't cure her?

Vaguely Janis noticed someone enter the room and sit down next to her. She glanced up through her tears and saw a young man wearing a short white shirt, probably an orderly. But why was he gazing at her with such tenderness? His eyes . . . they were so bright, so kind. Janis felt mesmerized.

"There's no need to cry," the man told her gently. "Your daughter is all right."

"I can't help it. I'm scared," Janis sobbed.

"You needn't be. She will grow up." He seemed definite about it. But the tests had just begun. How would he know the diagnosis already? Those eyes, that penetrating glance. . . . It was as if he was soothing her very soul. Janis seemed to be infused with grace, a sudden awareness that all would be well.

"I've looked at your child," the man said, getting up. "Don't be afraid. She's going to be fine." He put his hand on Janis's shoulder, then turned and walked out of the room.

Janis was alone again. But somehow, not alone. A presence seemed to linger in the room. She was filled with peace . . . she was happy! A few minutes later, her doctor came in and told her that the baby needed surgery right away.

Calmly Janis carried her infant to the surgical ward. Only later, when surgery was over and—just as predicted—the baby was thriving, did Janis attempt to locate the man in white who had so unexpectedly supported her. But no physician or orderly matched his description. Nor had any other parents been sent to the pediatric waiting room that morning. And hadn't he said he had *seen* her daughter?

Janis believes he did. And he still does.

"Have You Been Praying?"

*The most beautiful thing we can experience
is the mysterious.*

ALBERT EINSTEIN

*P*am and Ken Larson, of Ann Arbor, Michigan, wanted to adopt a baby. At the time, there were no private adoptions arranged in Michigan, and agencies would not consider them as clients, since they already had two children. So Pam and Ken looked elsewhere. They lived for a while in Spain, but failed to find a baby there. Ken, however, remained optimistic. "I'm sure we'll have another son someday," he told Pam upon their return from Spain. "And his name will be Michael."

Pam, a nurse, wasn't so sure, and her initial optimism was fading. Since before her marriage she had suffered recurring urinary-tract problems, which seemed to be getting worse. If they found a baby, would she be well enough to care for it? But when the Larsons met an attorney from Costa Rica who volunteered to help, Pam told him to try.

Pam and Ken completed the paperwork required for a foreign adoption, filled out forms for the immigration service, and went through a home study, planning to go to Costa Rica the moment the phone rang. But no word came. And Pam's health worsened. In 1984 she was diagnosed with interstitial cystitis, a degenerative bladder disease with no known cure.

"It was a difficult time for me," she says. "I believed God could heal people, but I thought of it sort of like the Irish Sweepstakes—I know someone wins, but since I don't buy tickets, it doesn't impact me." Pam had asked God for healing, and others had prayed over her too, but she remained sick—and discouraged.

In February 1985, a friend who had earlier prayed with Pam suggested her family pray over her again. Pam was reluctant—why would anything change now?—but she agreed. Afterward her condition was worse, but the next morning her family and friends prayed again. Her son Chris's hand began to tingle.

"Chris put his hand on my lower abdomen, and I felt a warmth come over me," Pam says. "Someone said, 'Look at her color!' My skin usually had a greenish tinge, but now I was turning pink." Within minutes Pam felt rejuvenated. Had she been healed?

In the midst of the joy and wonder of the next few days, the Larsons received a letter from the Costa Rican attorney. It had been three years since they'd asked him to help. Were they still interested in adopting? An eligible baby would be born in July.

Pam's health remained excellent as she prepared to live in Costa Rica for four to six weeks. When the call came that their son had been born, she was apprehensive about traveling alone to a foreign country, "with only my high school Spanish!" but she felt so well that she left all her medication behind.

Pam was given custody of the baby almost as soon as she arrived in Costa Rica, but nothing else went according to plan.

"Pages of documents would be lost or translated incorrectly, requiring extra work," she recalls. "My visa expired after thirty days, which meant I could be deported if caught. My biggest concern was that the baby's mother might change her mind." At one point the government revised some adoption laws and Pam was told the whole process might have to begin again.

Her lonely four-week vigil lengthened. Two months, three. . . . Ken came down to meet his new son and sign papers, but had to return to the children. Phone calls were a poor substitute for his reassuring presence. "I was depressed and fearful," Pam recalls. "Each day seemed like a month, and I often wept." But she prayed too. And despite the strain, her health remained perfect.

Finally, on November first, Pam's attorney presented her with all her legal documents. She and the baby could go home! Pam raced to a phone and called the U.S. Consulate. "I'd like to make an appointment to present the papers," she told the assistant U.S. Consul, Gabriella.

Gabriella went to get the file. "Mrs. Larson, you're missing one document, your final approval from U.S. Immigration," she said.

Another mix-up, on a paper that had been filed months ago! "We have a copy in Ann Arbor," Pam told her, trying to stay calm. "My husband can send it by special messenger."

"I'm sorry. We need the original. You'll have to refile in Washington."

"How long will that take?" Pam's voice was a whisper.

"Six weeks. At least."

Six weeks. Shocked, Pam hung up. How could this be happening, after all her work, her prayers? To leave the baby here was unthinkable. But to stay another day, another *moment?* She couldn't.

Pushing open the door, she went into the garage, an open structure surrounded by plants. Blindly, she paced, hardly aware of what she was doing. "God, have mercy," she prayed again and again. "Have mercy. . . ." She had come so far in her belief in Him, His love, His care. But now it seemed she would lose her hold on Him, would slip back into despair. . . .

And then she turned—and saw them. Two angels, two very large angels, so tall that she could see only their feet and ankles, until she bent down to look up. "They were barefoot," Pam says. "One was blond and holding a sword. I could see the tiny holes in the weave of his garment, the bottom of the rope belt that hung from his waist." She was stunned but, amazingly, unafraid.

"My name is Michael," one told her. "We're here to do battle for you."

Yes, she answered silently. *Of course.* Somehow, it seemed right. God would do this for her.

Pam had no sense of how long she stood there watching, marveling. Gradually, the vision faded. As it did, she had an overpowering urge to phone Gabriella again, although she had no idea what she would say.

But Gabriella was ecstatic. "Mrs. Larson, are you a Christian? Have you been praying?" she asked.

"Yes." Pam was still numb.

"And does God always answer your prayers this fast?"

Tears sprang to Pam's eyes. Something wonderful was happening. She knew it. "Lately He's been pretty quick, Gabriella. Why?"

"After you hung up, I turned around, and the messenger was standing here with a pouch," Gabriella explained. "And jammed in the bottom, under all the other papers, was your missing document."

We're here to do battle for you. . . .

"And we haven't been able to find your phone number . . ." Gabriella was still talking. "I'm so glad you called back. If you get here before we close, we can release you today!"

The incredible sequence seemed like a dream. Had heaven really intervened? But how else to explain it all?

Just a few days later Pam introduced her children to their new baby brother. Later she visited her urologist, who, astounded, pronounced her completely cured.

And as time passes, her answer to Gabriella's question becomes even more certain. Does Pam believe in prayer, in a God Who heals and sends angels and responds on His own perfect timetable? If she doubts, she need only look at her miracle child, her Michael, to find the answer.

Armchair Angel

Watch Thou, dear Lord, with those who wake, or watch, or weep tonight, and give thine angels charge over those who sleep.

SAINT AUGUSTINE

*J*ackie Commins, of Newberg, Oregon, is a firm believer in heavenly help. Since she doesn't own a car, she walks nearly two miles to work at the commercial laundry she manages. "Summers are fine, but our winters are rough, especially when you're traveling through ice and snow before dawn," she says. "But since I learned to ask God and His angels to be with me, I can actually feel unseen hands holding me up, especially on slippery spots."

One evening shortly after the New Year, however, Jackie learned even more dramatically how well God takes care of her. Because no heat gets to her bedroom, she sleeps on a couch in the living room during the winter. The couch is opposite her front door, and there is one window in the room—both open onto a small porch. Anyone on the porch can see directly into the room because curtains cover only the sides of the window.

Jackie was nearly asleep that evening when she was jolted by loud knocking at the door. Since she lives alone and all her lights were out, she decided not to answer. Whoever it was would surely go away.

However, the knocking continued, and now Jackie could hear the low voices of two men. They were talking on the other side of the door, just a few feet from her. Suddenly, one shone a flashlight through the window of the door, its ray narrowly missing her as she lay on the couch. Jackie's heart began to pound. These men were obviously up to no good.

Again, they murmured to each other, although she couldn't make out the words. Then she heard footsteps moving stealthily toward the window, and again the light went on. Its beam traveled slowly across the floor as far as it could go, then outlined Jackie's armchair, which directly faced the window. Just a thin pane of glass separated her from the intruders. "My God, my God. . . ." Frozen with fear, Jackie could find no other words for her prayer.

The light beam, which had been moving slowly across the armchair, suddenly stopped. Abruptly it clicked off, and Jackie heard one of the men talking excitedly to the other. The light went back on again, as if the second man was now holding the flashlight. Once again he focused the beam on the chair, then quickly extinguished it.

"Let's get out of here!" Jackie heard one of them exclaim, no longer attempting to be quiet. Two pairs of feet clattered across the porch to the staircase. In just a few seconds, there was silence. But it took Jackie several hours to fall asleep.

Days later, when Jackie read her weekly newspaper she learned what had happened on that terrifying night. Two men were in police custody, charged with burglarizing several houses in an area all around Jackie. The thugs had posed as travelers in distress, needing to use a phone. When kindly people opened the door, the men had overpowered them and robbed them of valuables and holiday gifts still under the tree. Obviously they had similar plans at Jackie's house. Except for one thing, the question that has intrigued her ever since.

What (or whom) did the men see sitting in the armchair?

Wonder at Wrigley Field

The farther we go along the path of God, the more angels we shall encounter.

DR. H. C. MOOLENBURGH, *A HANDBOOK OF ANGELS*

$\mathcal{A}$s Kenneth and Anita Steinke reared their six young children, it became obvious that Anita was the "spiritual one" in the family. "I had never been more than a Sunday Christian, with just a surface relationship with God," Kenneth says, and he saw no reason to change. But Anita prayed frequently that God would reveal Himself more deeply to her husband.

One afternoon Kenneth and Anita took the family to Wrigley Field, to watch the Chicago Cubs play the Cincinnati Reds. The Steinkes attended games often and considered themselves faithful Bleacher Bums, part of the crowd that overlooks the outfield. Bleacher seats were cheap, and families could bring picnics. And there was always the chance a Bum might catch a home-run ball.

Today the Steinkes sat in the right-field bleachers, with four-year-old Janet, the youngest, directly in front of Kenneth. "Janet was frail and small, but she enjoyed baseball," Kenneth says. Everyone was relaxed and upbeat.

Suddenly, in his mind, Kenneth heard words: "Janet is going to be hit in her temple with a fly ball. If you don't take action, she'll be seriously injured or killed."

Kenneth sat absolutely still, astounded. The message was so firm, so compelling that he never thought to doubt the truth of it. "It sounds strange, but I was convinced it was going to happen," he says.

How could he prepare? He could take Janet away. But the voice hadn't told him *when* the ball would come. Did it make sense to confine himself and his daughter in the car or to walk her around for the next several hours? And the other kids would be inconsolable if he insisted they go home now, especially on such flimsy-sounding evidence. But to Kenneth, the command was anything but frivolous.

What if he "rehearsed" for a fly ball? Slowly, unobtrusively, Kenneth slid his forearm in front of Janet's head. Yes, his arm was big enough to shield her. But could he react fast enough? For the next several minutes, Kenneth drilled himself, shoving his arm quickly in front of Janet, then releasing it, then shoving it again. . . .

Nearby fans began to notice his movements. Several looked at him strangely, perhaps wondering if he had developed some sort of tic. Janet was perplexed too. "What are you doing, Daddy?" she asked once. "I can't see!"

The crack of Pete Rose's bat was almost anticlimactic when it came just a few minutes later. The long line ball shot across the length of Wrigley Field like an arrow, picking up speed as it flew over the wall, right toward Janet's head. And in that split second, Kenneth knew just what to do. Throwing his left arm across his daughter's forehead, just as he'd practiced, he used his right hand to shield his own face. The ball struck his arm with a terrible force, bounced off, bounced on and off Anita, then disappeared into a pile of people.

Kenneth looked at his left arm. It was already starting to swell. But Janet was safe, her little face still whole and perfect.

Kenneth stayed up late that night. His arm throbbed, but it wasn't the pain that kept him awake. What had happened today? Had he really received a message from Janet's guardian angel, or his? Or had it been simply a father's intuition?

Then Kenneth remembered another episode, a few years ago. In a frightening dream, he had seen his toddler son, Kenny, sliding down a muddy embankment while he, Kenneth, grabbed the child with one hand, and held on to a tree with the other. "Kenny is going to drown unless you save him," a voice told him in the dream. Kenneth had awakened in alarm, but later dismissed his fears.

The day after the dream, however, he had taken the five older children out for a ride. "We drove rather aimlessly, until we got to a nature area where I used to play as a child," he recalls. "We walked along a trail, and as we turned a corner, there was a river with a dam just ahead."

"Daddy, look!" Kenny ran toward the water, and Kenneth ran after him. Rivers were no place for impulsive tots. But Kenny began to slide down a muddy incline—right toward the whirling vortex of the dam.

"Look out!" Kenneth shouted, leaning forward to grasp the little boy.

"I had him with one hand and was reaching for a tree to steady myself, when all of a sudden I realized that the scene was right out of my dream," Kenneth says. "I had been there just when I needed to be, to keep Kenny from falling and being pulled under the water." God *must* be calling him closer. What more proof did Kenneth need?

Today Kenneth's relationship with God is a priority. And he's glad he has had angels in his life—both the heavenly and earthly variety—who never lost faith in him.

The Vanishing
Lifeguard

All night, all day,
Angels watching over me, my Lord. . . .

"ALL NIGHT, ALL DAY," TRADITIONAL SONG

*L*ike many parents, Carla Rizzuto often asks her children's guardian angels to protect them in a general way. But twice, she has received very specific answers.

When Paul was about four, a pediatric cardiologist discovered a hole in his heart. "On rare occasions a hole closes by itself," the doctor told Carla. "But such a thing would take years, and Paul will need surgery soon." His two partners looked at the tests and concurred. Carla went home to pray. She asked God to put Paul's angel in charge of the situation and to keep her little boy healthy.

Five months later, as Paul's tests were repeated in preparation for surgery, the doctor was startled to see a perfect heart. "We just don't have an answer," he told Carla.

Carla smiled at him. "I do," she said.

Three years later, the Rizzutos visited Disney World's water park in Florida. They were having a wonderful time. All afternoon they had climbed to the top of the water chute and plummeted down into the lake in their rafts. Carla and her husband, Andy, always went before Paul. "The lake was deep at the end of the slide, and since Paul couldn't swim, we wanted to be ahead of him in case he fell out of the inner tube," Carla explains.

At one point, Carla pushed off with Paul behind. But as they sped into a wider lane, she was astonished to see him tear by, revolving wildly. His raft had caught in a groove and was out of control.

Paul looked tiny—and terrified. "Paul, hang on to the handles!" Carla called as she tried to reach him. But her tube was spinning too, and she lost sight of him for a few seconds. As she shot toward the lake, her heart almost stopped.

Paul's empty raft was bobbing nearby. But there was no sign of her son.

"Paul!" Carla cried. Quickly she dove. The water was just a bit over her head, not terribly deep, but murky. She couldn't see Paul. She surfaced for a moment, frantically searching the area around her. Where was he? Just then she felt something hit her leg.

Again she went under. Paul! She gripped him tightly, but as she tried to pull him up to the surface, he started to struggle. "He was panicking and dragging me down," Carla says. "I didn't know if anyone had seen us, and I was as scared as he was."

She wouldn't let go of Paul. But Carla's lungs were ready to burst. She couldn't stay under and hold him much longer. Suddenly she felt a pair of strong hands grip her waist from under the water and push her up. Still clinging to Paul, she broke through the surface, safe! Who had grabbed her? She looked into the calm, serene face of a man treading water.

He was young, with curly brown hair. Probably the lifeguard.

"Oh, thank you!" But as Carla turned to Paul, she saw that the lifeguard was on the pier and had just thrown a life preserver to her son. Confused, she looked back.

Their rescuer wasn't there.

"Where did he go?" Confused, Carla scanned the shore, but no one was swimming back. There was no man near the pier where the lifeguard stood watching. No one at all who looked anything like their rescuer.

"Who, Mommy?" Paul was quickly reviving. By now Andy had come down the chute and was bobbing toward them on his raft.

"The man, honey. The one who pushed us out of the water just now."

Paul frowned. "I didn't see any man," he said.

Paul and Andy went over to the pier. Carla slowly made her way to shore, then sat for a while. Her emotions were in turmoil. The more she thought about the near miss, the more frightened she was. Yet, underlying her anxiety was a sense of tranquillity, almost giddiness, a feeling she wanted to savor and enjoy. She stared at the water. Who had the man been? Why hadn't he stayed nearby so she could thank him properly? And there was something else odd about the incident, something Carla couldn't quite identify.

Of course! She sat bolt upright. The man had been submerged, for Carla had felt his hands *pushing* her from underneath.

But when she had looked into his face, his curly brown hair had been completely dry.

"God is always taking care of us," Carla says, "and the best gift He's given me is my faith in Him, the faith to keep asking, and keep looking each day for the blessings He sends."

Miracle Miles

"See, I am sending an angel ahead of you to guard
you along the way . . ."

EXODUS 23:20

It was July 1983, and trucker Michael Harrington had just
started a new job, dispatched out of Dakota City, Nebraska,
with a load of beef destined for Birmingham, Alabama. On
the way, Michael's truck had electrical problems, so when he
reached the terminal in West Memphis, Arkansas, he pulled in
to exchange tractors.

"I was a little leery of lowering the landing gear on the trailer,"
Michael says. "Earlier in the year, when I worked for another
company, I had done the same thing and the handle had given
way." Thrown off balance, Michael had fallen and dislocated
his right knee, eventually requiring surgery.

So Michael lowered this load with extra care. But as he
steadied himself and turned the crank one more time—it happened again! The jack gave way and Michael fell.

Searing pain rolled over him. In horror, he realized that he
had dislocated his *left* knee—and it would have to be reset. But
how? He was in a strange area—how could he find a doctor

now? Or should he try to do it himself? Aware of the long journey still ahead, Michael gritted his teeth, slowly put his left knee in between the tandem tires, turned onto his right side, and pulled as hard as he could.

With a sickening snap, the kneecap popped back into place, but immediately his leg began to swell. The pain was agonizing. Holding the side of the truck, Michael dragged himself to his feet and hobbled to a chair. *The company will have to put me on a plane for home,* he thought. *There's no way I can finish this trip now.*

The dispatcher had other ideas. "You're the only driver we've got, Michael, and the beef you're hauling is worth over two hundred and fifty thousand dollars," he said. "I'll do my best to get you home from Birmingham, but you've got to go on."

Under normal circumstances, it takes good arms, good legs and eyes, and plenty of muscle power to drive a huge truck. But as Michael crawled into the cab, he was screaming on the inside. How was he going to shift gears? He knew how to upshift and downshift without using a clutch. "But you need a clutch when you first take off, and I didn't know what to do about that," he says. His leg seemed to be on fire.

Sitting in his truck, Michael felt hopeless. He bowed his head. *God,* he prayed silently, *I don't have the strength to complete this job. Please send an angel to be my guide.*

Slowly Michael drove the remaining miles to Birmingham, stopping along the way to sleep. Exhausted, he pulled into the terminal, and after unloading the beef, he phoned the company doctor and his dispatcher in Arkansas to make arrangements to get home. "By now my leg was so swollen that I couldn't get the pant leg off, and it was starting to shut off my circulation," Michael says. "I knew I was in serious trouble."

But there was no end in sight. For although the company doctor didn't want Michael driving, the dispatcher was in a bind. "We can't bring your truck home empty," he told Michael. "The best we can do is to send you to Ringgold, Georgia. You can switch loads with another trucker there, and go on to Fort Smith, Arkansas. From there, we can get you home." Michael had no choice but to agree.

Somehow he made it to Ringgold and switched loads. But his leg was now about three times its normal size. And as Michael pulled out on the interstate and headed for Nashville at about ten P.M., he was desperate. How was he going to pull a forty-ton load in this condition?

"I remember thinking about our POWs in North Vietnam," Michael says. "What kept them going? What held their spirit together when they were suffering and they knew it would be a long time before they saw home?" Michael felt that he was a prisoner in his truck. Only willpower—and God's help—would sustain him.

But about midnight as he reached Monteagle, Tennessee, he began to deteriorate. "This is some of the prettiest country anywhere," he says. "They say it took God six days to create the world. My guess is that, when He rested, it was in Monteagle."

Usually Michael loved climbing Monteagle Hill, flying up at sixty miles an hour. But this time he pulled into the slow lane and kept a forty-five-miles-per-hour speed, feeling more light-headed with each tire revolution. Dizzy, nauseated, and perspiring, he felt as if his heart were pounding out of his chest. "God," he cried out again, his leg burning, "please help me! Get me down safely!"

It seemed an impossible plea. Surely he would black out and lose control of his rig. But as he reached the very summit of Monteagle Hill, Michael was suddenly flooded with peace. It was bliss, reassurance that filled him to the brim, a certainty that everything was going to be all right—and that he was no longer in control of his truck. It was the last thing he remembered.

For when Michael again became aware of his surroundings, he was driving into the eastern edge of Memphis, some three hundred miles from Monteagle Hill. His hands were still on the steering wheel, and everything seemed normal. Except. . . . Michael checked his watch. Six hours had passed.

Stunned, he pulled over to the side of the highway. Six hours! He had crossed half of Tennessee in a fully loaded tractor-trailer, and he didn't remember anything! Grabbing his CB radio, he asked fellow truckers if they knew of any accidents between Monteagle Hill and Memphis. None did.

"I've been right behind you," one driver radioed. "What's the problem?"

"I . . . haven't been feeling well the past few hours," Michael tried to explain. "Was anything wrong with my driving?"

"Not a thing," the other driver answered. "You changed lanes just fine."

Changed lanes! Driving a forty-ton rig! And somehow he had even chosen the right roads to circle the congestion at Nashville.

Or . . . had he chosen anything at all? Michael remembered his agony, his desolate plea for help. "God," he whispered in awe, "did You send an angel to drive my truck for me?" Tears ran down his cheeks as the first rays of the sun peeked over the horizon, warming him through to his bones.

A postscript: Michael made it home safely, had knee surgery, and prepared for his October wedding. When the day arrived, however, he was still on crutches. Determined to go through the ceremony without them, he felt confident—except for the three steps leading to the altar in the little Presbyterian chapel. Could he climb them on his own?

"I was pretty shaky that morning, but I stood without crutches in the front as Brenda, my fiancée, came down the aisle," he says. "I had my cousin as best man standing right next to me, in case I started to fall."

The tricky moment arrived. Michael turned, took Brenda's arm to steady himself, and carefully began to climb the steps. Just then he felt another arm grasp him and help him up. "I turned to tell my cousin that it was okay, that I could manage alone," Michael says.

But the beaming best man was standing at least ten feet behind Michael. And no one else was close enough to have touched him. No one visible, that is.

Today Michael still occasionally senses God's presence. But even on darker days, he walks in faith, knowing that angels are always near.

Summons to the
Danger Zone

*O Guardian Angel, cover me with thy wing; O Friend,
illumine my path. Direct my footsteps and be my
protection, just for today.*

SAINT THERESE OF LISIEUX

*N*urse Edie Murphy worked at a state psychiatric hospital
in Massachusetts. Such a job is always challenging, and one of
the hardest parts, Edie says, is admitting new patients being
brought in by ambulance. "You're never sure what state they're
in, if they're violent, for instance," she says. Ambulances at
that hospital discharged patients in a basement area, somewhat
deserted and removed from regular hospital activity. Because of
this, proper procedure involved *two* people meeting the ambulance, an admitting nurse accompanied by a male mental-health
technician.

One night Edie was helping out in a ward other than her own,
when she learned that a patient was on his way by ambulance.
Because everyone else was busy, Edie volunteered to meet him.
"I was uneasy because I rarely did Admissions, and the technician

who accompanied me was new and very hesitant," she says. However, as the two came down the quiet corridor, Edie saw Dan* waiting for them. This was a relief, since Dan was a strong and thoroughly reliable tech with whom she had often worked, though never in Admissions. What a nice coincidence that he happened to be there at just the right moment!

Before she could ask Dan why he was working night duty, the ambulance drove up, deposited the patient, and left.

"Hi, I'm Edie Murphy." Edie smiled at the young man who she later learned was psychotic. "I'll be doing your admission." She watched as his expression began to change. This could be a dangerous point, when a patient realized he was going to be hospitalized.

Without warning, the young man lunged at Edie, grabbing for her throat. The other tech barely reacted, but Dan, instantly alert, caught the patient in a basket hold and subdued him while Edie summoned additional help.

Her heart was still racing an hour later when she and Dan had a chance to discuss the close call. "I'm so glad you were there," Edie told him. "Otherwise, I could have been badly injured."

"It was lucky you phoned," Dan agreed. "But how did you know I was working overtime, and five buildings away from you?"

Edie frowned. "What do you mean, Dan? I didn't call you."

"But. . . ." Dan stared at her, puzzled. "Some woman phoned our medical-room nurse. She said, 'Send Dan to Admissions. Edie needs help.' "

Some woman. . . . But who? The busy nurses on Edie's floor hadn't phoned. They had already sent an escort with Edie, and they weren't aware Dan was still on duty, in a building on the other side of the grounds. The nurse on Dan's ward didn't know Edie or anything about a new admission. When the phone rang, that nurse was in the usually vacant cubbyhole, pouring a medication.

Who summoned Dan to the danger zone before Edie had even arrived? No one ever discovered the answer.

"The Ninety-first Psalm about angelic protection has always been a favorite of mine," Edie says. "But on that day, several others became believers too!"

Christmas Messenger

Angels may not always come when you call them, but they come when you need them.

KAREN GOLDMAN, *THE ANGEL BOOK*

In the early 1970s, a congregation in Rockford, Illinois, bought some farmland in order to build a church and a Christian radio station. They erected a little house that would shelter the station temporarily—if it ever got launched.

Starting the station required just the right person, Pastor Don Lyons knew—someone sharing the community's spiritual views, but with a professional background in the media. As he prayed about it, from time to time, the pastor would see the name *Tietsort* spelled out in his mind. It was such an unusual name—one he had never heard—that he was inclined to dismiss it as imagination.

One day, however, the churches in Rockford hosted a pastors' meeting, inviting clergy from all around the state. Pastor Lyons was greeting guests when a young man stepped up to introduce himself. When Pastor Lyons saw his nametag, his mouth dropped. The young man's name was Ron Tietsort. Not only was Ron a pastor, but he also had had a radio and television ministry in Sioux City, Iowa. Soon Ron accepted the job of station manager, and moved his wife, Millie, and their family to Rockford.

Station WQFL began to broadcast, but keeping it on the air was a financial struggle, and Ron found it difficult to meet the monthly bills. Because the station was a spiritual venture, he ran few paid commercials, at least at first. "We wanted to wait upon the Lord," Ron explains. "We believed that if He was blessing this project, He would supply most of our needs through donations."

While Ron coped with management duties and hired a small staff, Millie acted as part-time receptionist, bookkeeper, and occasional programmer. "We wore a lot of hats," she says, "but it was a labor of love."

However, as the winter of 1975 approached, Ron and Millie had to face reality. Despite their dedication, long hours, and prayers, WQFL was in financial trouble. Their listener base was definitely increasing. Fund-raisers were frequent and profitable, but revenues weren't keeping pace with expenses. They had fallen behind a little each month, and one afternoon when Millie did the books she came to a grim conclusion. In order to catch up and keep going, WQFL needed just over three thousand dollars—now.

It might as well have been three million. Millie sat in her receptionist chair next to the little house's front window, gazed upon a new snowfall on the silent fields—and wanted to cry. Christmas was approaching, but for her and Ron, it seemed the end rather than a hopeful beginning. All their hard work, the dreams shared by the founding congregation—everything seemed to be sinking in a mass of debt.

God, Millie prayed, *we really thought You wanted the station to succeed. Did we misread You? Please tell us what to do now.*

The room remained silent, its hush seemingly magnified by the stark whiteness outside. No one had come by all day. How she wished for company now, a friendly neighbor to comfort her, even a delivery person bringing a touch of Christmas into the little room.

As if in answer to her unspoken plea, the front door opened, and a middle-aged man strode in, carrying a sealed envelope. Millie was surprised. She had heard no car coming up the long driveway, no footsteps on the porch, as she usually did. But perhaps the new snow had muffled the sounds. She smiled at the man. Although she knew many townspeople by now, she had never seen him before.

The man handed her the envelope. "Give this to Ron," he told her. "Use it for the station."

"This is very kind of you," she said. "Would you like to talk to Ron? I can call him."

"That won't be necessary," the man answered.

It was not unusual for people to pop by with a donation—in a way, the station belonged to everyone in the town. But usually benefactors stayed for a while to chat. This brusque man was already turning away, although he would need a receipt for tax purposes. "Just a minute, and I'll—" Millie began, but the stranger closed the door behind him.

Strange, she thought again.

She walked back to Ron's desk and laid the envelope in front of him. Absently he slit it open, then gasped. "Millie, look!"

Inside was cash. Just over three thousand dollars.

Ron leaped from his chair and raced to the front of the house. Who would give them this much money—and without a receipt? It must have been a mistake, a mix-up in envelopes! The stranger would be devastated when he discovered his error. Ron flung open the front door, to call the man back.

But there was no car parked in front of the little dwelling, in fact, there were no tire tracks traced in the driveway—none coming down from the road and none going back. Ron's astonished gaze fell on the snow-covered porch, the steps leading away from it, the front walk. He hadn't shoveled yet, but there were no footprints marring the white carpet. It lay in unbroken smoothness across the entire landscape, as far as Ron could see.

Today WQFL and its sister station WGSL are owned by the First Assembly of God Church in Rockford, and Millie and Ron have watched their long-ago dreams come true. Neither ever saw the stranger again. But sometimes, especially during the Christmas season, they hear the whisper of wings. And they remember.

BOOK THREE

~~

MIRACLES
FROM
BEYOND

When Loved Ones Come

I used to think my deceased husband was my "angel," and that he was always with me for protection. Now I know my husband and my guardian angel are working as a team.

IRIS CALOGERO, A READER FROM SLIDELL, LOUISIANA

$\mathcal{A}$t her husband's funeral, Mary impulsively took a pink carnation from a floral arrangement and laid it on the coffin. Weeks later, while trudging down a snow-covered street, a wave of grief rolled over her. "Oh, Tom," she murmured, "if only I could know that you are in God's arms!"

Suddenly Mary stopped. There on the frozen sidewalk in front of her lay a pink carnation.

Jim, following a lifelong dream, had started a monthly newspaper. While printing the first issue, he thought of his father, who had died several years ago. He wished he could talk over his plans with Dad.

Then, out of the corner of his eye, Jim sensed a presence. A man wearing a plaid lumberjack shirt, the kind his father had always liked, seemed to be standing next to him. Instead of being afraid, Jim felt serene. But when he turned to face the figure, it disappeared.

For the next several months, the man in the plaid shirt briefly appeared—just out of Jim's line of vision—on the evenings Jim printed his paper. One night, after circulation had increased and Jim felt more confident, he started the press and realized he was alone. Jim understood. He had wished for a father's special touch at the beginning of his venture, and God had answered his prayer.

Driving home from work in a blizzard, Harry* was startled to see on his windshield the face of his grandmother, who had died many years ago. The face seemed to be alive, just as he remembered her. In Yiddish, the language they both shared, she said to him, "Go where I'm sending you."

Harry feared he was losing his mind. Yet he stepped on the gas obediently and drove blindly, unable to see more than a few feet ahead. The vision on the windshield faded.

The car seemed to turn corners and steer itself, but eventually it stopped—in front of the house where Harry's mother and sister lived. Incredulous, he rang the bell. When his mother opened the door, she burst into tears.

"Thank God you've come!" she sobbed. "Your sister is unconscious, and the phone isn't working because of the storm."

Harry drove his sister to the hospital, where doctors discovered that she had diabetes and had lapsed into a coma. Her life was saved because a grandmother's love had somehow spanned both distance and time.

Are these angel experiences? Many people wrote that a loved one seemed so close after death that "she has become my guardian angel." Do people become angels after they die?

There is nothing in Scripture or tradition supporting the idea that humans ever turn into angels, despite popular movie and novel plots. Jesus referred to those who have entered heaven as being "like the angels," (Luke 20:36), not angels in fact. Nor have angels ever been human, although they may occasionally assume human likeness. Instead, angels and humans are parallel creations, each unique, with their own characteristics. Although the two certainly interact, they do not *become* one another.

Does this mean that visions of or touches from loved ones who have died are nothing more than delusions or wishful thinking? Not at all. In the Catholic tradition, such things go on all the time, via officially recognized saints. To Catholics, a saint is similar to a fond aunt or uncle, an older, wiser family member who can advise or intercede in certain matters. Some saints are known for specific causes, and the list is always growing, due to the canonization process.

However, Catholics and most other Christians believe that *everyone* in heaven is sanctified. Thus, if loved ones prayed for us while they were on earth, isn't it logical that they would continue their vigilance and intercession from paradise? And wouldn't we occasionally sense their presence?

Such connections probably occur more often than we realize. In 1973, the National Opinion Research Center at the University of Chicago asked the question, "Have you ever felt you were in touch with someone who died?" A surprising 27% of those polled said "yes." When widows and widowers were added to the sample, the proportion rose to 51%. The survey was repeated in 1984, with even higher numbers, including 38% of teenagers reporting such happenings. "Those who believe in life after death, who pray frequently and who regard God more as a lover than a judge" are more likely to have such encounters, says Father Andrew Greeley in an article based on this data.

In addition, many of the more than five million Americans

claiming to have had near-death experiences reported seeing deceased relatives and friends, as well as that glorious Being of Light. After all, although we think of paradise as a place "above," it may actually be as near as a heartbeat. "[T]he kingdom of God is within you," Jesus said (Luke 17:21). Why wouldn't those who have already entered the kingdom be just as close to us as He?

We must remember, however, that there is a clear boundary between a *spontaneous* and unexpected contact with someone in heaven (such as the Transfiguration) and attempts to "summon spirits" with séances, Ouija boards, witchcraft, or other dark practices. "The Bible warns seriously against making contact with the dead through a medium," says H. C. Moolenburgh, Dutch physician and author of *Meetings with Angels*.

"Miracles have a divine purpose," adds Father Robert DeGrandis, S.S.J., author and teacher. "Searching for power apart from God can lead a person into an occult approach to knowledge, which is dangerous."

God knows the depths of our heartache and loneliness, how much we long to be reassured that our loved ones are in His care. As we remain open to His will and timing, He may send comfort just when we most need it, from those who live on the other side of the veil, in the Eternal Light.

A Rainbow
from Andy

~~

Think of him still as the same, I say,
He is not dead; he is just—away.

JAMES WHITCOMB RILEY,
"HE IS NOT DEAD"

When eleven-year-old Andy Bremner came home from a camp for cancer patients, he brought a little sun-catcher for his mother, Linda. It was a plastic rainbow, one of her favorite symbols. Linda barely glanced at the gift, however. A Wisconsin hospital had just informed her that Andy was a candidate for a bone-marrow transplant, and she was intent on packing quickly. She had no idea how long they would be staying, but the sooner she got her sick son on the road toward hope, the better she would feel.

In Wisconsin, Linda rented a small apartment, but she spent most hours at the hospital, first cheering Andy on through his transplant, later sitting anxiously by his bed. She prayed for his healing, as she had done constantly since the beginning of his illness. But God remained silent, the aloof, faraway God of her childhood. And although the transplant was successful, the preceding four years of chemotherapy and radiation had taken a toll on Andy. Instead of growing stronger, he seemed to slip further away.

One morning, desperate for something to interest Andy and keep his mind off his increasing pain, Linda browsed through the hospital gift shop and found a prism, a little light-reflecting ornament. "Here's a rainbow-maker, Andy," she said as she presented it to him. "Now you can make one for me!"

Weakly Andy surveyed the prism. "I don't feel like it, Mom," he said, letting it fall out of his limp fingers.

"Sure you do, Andy," Linda pressed him. "Come on. Hold it up to the sun and make one for me, please?"

Andy's eyes were half closed. "Mom," he murmured, "someday I'll make you a rainbow like you've never seen before."

"That's great, honey!" Linda tried to sound enthusiastic, but Andy had already fallen asleep.

Days dragged by, and Andy got thinner. He had been put on a respirator, and toward the end of his seventh week in the hospital, he became comatose and was taken to Intensive Care. Linda phoned family members and asked them to come to Wisconsin. The time was drawing near.

Andy was unconscious for a week, but Linda stayed near him constantly, still hoping for a miracle. "God, heal him," she continued to pray. "I'll do anything . . . anything You ask." But God seemed elsewhere.

Just before dawn on the morning of August 31, Andy's breaths grew further and further apart. One of his physicians had come, and now he spoke gently to Linda. "If you consent, we can take Andy off life supports."

No! Linda knew there had been brain seizures, that the child she had known was forever gone. But if God gave her a miracle right now, if He spared her son's life, she'd take Andy in *any* condition. *God, please!* But God didn't answer.

It was dark in the room, and for the first time since Andy had slipped into a coma, Linda reached to open the blinds to the grayness outside. "I want to see the sun when it comes," she told the doctor and her gathering family. As the blinds parted, Linda saw mounted on the glass the same kind of rainbow sun-catcher that Andy had brought her from camp. Oh, that had been such a hopeful day, with the transplant—and possible cure—waiting just ahead!

But the dream was over. Now, sitting in the bedside chair where she'd been for this seemingly endless week, Linda gathered her frail son into her arms. "Fight, Andy!" she started to whisper. "Come on, you can do it—"

But even as she formed the words, she knew that it wasn't the right message anymore. "Oh, Andy!" Tearfully, she cuddled him and whispered through the semidarkness. "You've fought hard enough. Now it's time for all of us to let go. Go home now, honey. Go home."

For just a moment after his tubes were disconnected, Andy continued to breathe. One breath, two . . . and then silence. Linda felt a sense of surrender. *He's Yours now, God,* she thought.

Suddenly, as the rising sun peeked over the hill, its light hit the little ornament on the window. And in a glorious burst of color, the plastic rainbow multiplied, becoming four, eight, thirty rainbows, filling the room with brilliance and life. Like a joyful explosion, the arches danced, bounced, leaping through the plastic tubes, swirling across the blanket in a kaleidoscope of reds and blues and greens, as if God had sent a million prisms to magnify His rays. The display went on and on, as everyone stared in amazement. It was . . . a rainbow like Linda had never seen before.

"In that moment," she says now, "I said good-bye to Andy, and hello to God, perhaps for the first time. He wasn't Someone out of a book, or Someone my parents had told me about. Now He was mine. He had taken Andy to a better place, and He was going to be with me always. He had just told me so."

Several weeks later, Linda was cleaning out Andy's drawers when she found a little address book with a list of other kids at the cancer camp. Remembering how much Andy had liked getting mail when he was sick, Linda stood for a moment holding the book. What if she wrote a cheerful note to each child, as a sort of legacy to Andy? She was still thinking about it the next day when her mail came, bearing a colorful sympathy card from a friend, with a line that read, *You're welcome to share my rainbow.*

Linda remembered Andy's multicolored path into heaven. She reached for a sheet of paper and began to write.

Today, Love Letters reaches over one thousand chronically ill children every month with cards, little toys, and love, especially love, from Linda, the friends who help her . . . and from Andy, whose rainbow started it all.[5]

From Darkness
to Light

*You live through the darkness from what you learned
in the light.*

HOPE MACDONALD, *WHEN ANGELS APPEAR*

𝒫aula Trapalis's father had a heart attack in November 1991, and although it was a fearful time for the family, he seemed to recover. The following June, however, he developed ominous new symptoms and went to the hospital. On the night preceding his tests, Paula had what she describes as "a dreamlike experience. I know it was not actually a dream, but somehow I saw a light, which left me with a sad impression about my dad." There were no words, no actual vision. Paula just sensed that something unfortunate was going to happen.

The test results were not good. Paula's father had cancer. During the next months as he underwent treatment, Paula avoided thinking about the curious light. If it had been a message, it was not one she wanted to hear.

Paula was also apprehensive because she was getting married on Saturday, August 22, 1992. Her dad loved her fiancé, Tony, and had been looking forward to the wedding. "Dad, you have to get well in time," Paula teased her father at the hospital, "because if you don't walk me down the aisle, I won't go!"

Her father teased her right back. But on Monday, August 17, he died.

Paula was in anguish. Not only did she mourn her father's loss, this extraordinary timing made everything even worse. Wednesday night after the funeral, she fell into bed exhausted and tormented. She couldn't possibly marry Tony on Saturday. She'd have to call off the wedding.

Paula had been sleeping restlessly for several hours, when suddenly she awakened. There, again, was the light that had come to her several months ago. "It was brighter than the sun, coming from the ceiling, saturating the dark room from the top down," Paula says. But instead of sorrow, she felt an indescribable jubilance. The light filled her, wrapping her with warmth and reassurance, soothing her broken heart as she watched it, welcomed it, *basked* in it. "I got a message, though not in words, that I should go on, and everything would be all right."

The next thing she remembers is her dog bounding into the room and the light going out. "The dog was shaking and frightened, the way she acts in a storm," Paula says. But the night was clear.

How long had she been in touch with the light? Paula had no idea if a minute or several hours had passed. But now she slept peacefully, and the next day she told her mother about what had happened.

"That's strange . . ." Paula's mother murmured.

"Why, Mom?"

"Because—I know this will sound odd—last night I felt a hand on my shoulder while I was in bed." Like Paula, her mother had been filled with bliss.

Paula was joyful on her wedding day. Joyful and astonished. How could she feel like this, she wondered, when just five days earlier, her whole world had collapsed? And yet, she was happy. It was as if her father were still with her, lending her his support and pride and filling her with . . . light.

Paula has often prayed for the light to return, but she suspects it won't, at least not for a long time. Nor has she yet come to a conclusion about what the light really was. Her father? An angel? Whatever brought it, Paula is certain that it was a message from heaven, sent just when she, Tony, and her family needed it most. "Even today I carry with me that inner peace, and the ability to 'hold it together,' even though I miss Dad terribly," she says. "I believe there are signs like this all around us. It's just a matter of accepting them for what they really are."

Between Heaven
and Earth

*Although the span from earth to heaven is a journey
of five hundred years, when one whispers a prayer, or
even silently meditates, God is nearby and hears.*

BIBLICAL COMMENTARY BY RABBAH,
AN ANCIENT JEWISH SAGE

𝒜s the youngest of three girls, Chris Costello of Burbank,
California, had always tried to "catch up" to her middle sister,
Carole. The two experienced much sibling rivalry through
adolescence and young adulthood. "There were those long
and sometimes painful stretches when, due to an argument,
Carole and I would not talk to each other. Instead, each of
us would go to our oldest sister for advice and consolation,"
Chris recalls. Both girls shared music as a bond, however, and
though they never performed together, each worked for a while
as a professional singer.

In 1987, Carole and Chris reached a turning point, and old
conflicts no longer really mattered. "One night we just sat and
talked," Chris recalls. "For the first time we were able to look
at each other and share our love." The evening brought much

healing. And it had come just in time, for three months later, Carole suddenly died of a brain aneurysm.

In the days that followed the funeral, Chris was inconsolable, her grief complicated by the realization that she and Carole had wasted precious time. "I walked around like a zombie," she says. "All I really wanted was to know that Carole was okay." Once she seemed to sense the aroma of Carole's perfume enfolding her. On another occasion, she had a dream in which Carole appeared, smiling and happy, and told Chris she loved her. These little signs soothed Chris. But did they really mean anything?

At least a month later, Chris was still raw. One night as she lay in bed, she murmured again and again, "Please, Carole, give me a sign that you're okay."

Suddenly, Chris felt a bright light. She shut her eyes tighter and put her arm over them. But the light became more intense, penetrating through her arm, her closed eyes, wrapping her in its brilliance.

Chris was afraid. "In my mind, I begged whatever it was to go away—I didn't want to open my eyes and see some sort of apparition," she says. At her plea, the light slowly faded, and everything returned to normal.

But now Chris felt ashamed. She had asked for a sign from Carole, then refused to acknowledge it. Had God sent that unusual radiance to answer her prayer, to let her know that her sister was safe and happy?

A few nights later, Chris awakened—at exactly three-twenty A.M.—to beautiful celestial music wafting through her darkened bedroom. The music was exquisite, indescribable, involving "instrumentation I have never heard before, could never begin to define, despite my musical background," she says. "Even with all the high-tech equipment available now in recording studios, I doubt anyone could duplicate it." Chris listened, enthralled and moved to tears. Was this Carole, communicating with her through music, their closest tie?

The next morning, Chris's oldest sister phoned. "Chris, last night I sensed Carole's presence all around me," she said. "She was there—she was okay—I just know it!"

"What time did this happen?" Chris asked.

"Exactly three-twenty."

Chris felt her sorrow drain away and a newfound sense of peace replace it. Carole was indeed singing with the angels and had sent her a taste of wonders unseen.

Is there such a thing as heavenly music? Betty Malz, author of *Angels Watching Over Me,* has an audio tape of a small congregation in London singing an "Alleluia." As they sang, the people realized that the song was growing in magnitude and range. They were being accompanied by a massive unseen choir! When they replayed the tape, a music teacher found that the highest notes were almost three octaves above middle C, far out of human range.[6]

Evangelists Charles and Frances Hunter witnessed something similar while conducting a service in Austin, Texas. They had just asked the prayer leader to lead the large audience in song without accompaniment when, from the direction of the empty piano bench, they heard what sounded like a thousand-piece orchestra tuning instruments. The volume increased, and just as the prayer leader started to sing, the whole invisible orchestra broke into harmony and played along. "What an awesome experience for us and him, as we heard the music of a thousand angels!" Charles exclaimed.[7]

Many readers told me of hearing unexpected, unexplainable music, especially at the time of a death. But they have usually kept silent about it, fearing others would assume it was a grief-induced hallucination. Michelle

Crossley, however, didn't hesitate to share what happened to her.

At three o'clock one morning, Michelle's phone rang. It was her husband's sister, calling with bad news.

"Is it your mom?" Michelle immediately asked. Tim's mother had been going through a crisis.

"No—it's our cousin Brian,*" Michelle's sister-in-law said. "Michelle, he's dead. He was playing the guitar with his band tonight—and he just collapsed."

Tim's cousin Brian! But he was their dear friend as well as a relative, just twenty-three, a year younger than she. Shocked, Michelle handed the phone to her husband. Then she went into the living room and wept. Tim came after her and began to cry too.

Michelle reached for her Bible and read aloud from Ecclesiastes. "There is a time for everything, and a season for every activity under heaven: a time to be born and a time to die. . . ." The words seemed to comfort Tim a little. Michelle was calmer too. Brian—they would never see him again, not here on earth, anyway. It was almost too much to absorb.

Then another thought intruded. Had Brian gone to heaven? "All of a sudden it was the only question I could ask," Michelle says. "I wanted to know where he was now. In fact, I didn't think I could handle *not* knowing."

She hesitated to share her thoughts with her grief-striken husband, so her prayer was a silent one. *Lord, please tell me where Brian is. Please send me a sign. Please. Please. . . .*

Minutes passed. Michelle continued to pray, and eventually Tim got up to check their three sleeping toddlers. As soon as he left the room, it happened.

"I started to hear beautiful singing, music that was coming from some other kind of plane," Michelle says. "I knew the tune—we sing it at Calvary Chapel, and it's called 'A Shield

About Me.' " Voices were singing it word-perfect. And the fullness, the range! "It was exquisite. I knew angels had come to tell me that Brian was home."

The music continued for several minutes, then gradually grew fainter. Michelle was flooded with peace, love, and faith. "Oh, Tim!" she whispered when he came back. "You'll never guess what just happened!"

Awed, Tim listened to her explanation, and wept again, this time in relief.

Later, the young couple was able to comfort their entire family, bringing assurance that Brian was in heaven. "God has touched me in so many ways," Michelle says. "I can't wait to meet Jesus face-to-face, and hear those angels sing again!"

Lights and music are not the only means by which God sends comfort to us at a time of sorrow. Several people shared stories of unexplained aromas, usually flowers but also fragrant perfume, as Chris Costello experienced. "I thought the scent of lilac powder suddenly flooding the car's interior must be coming through the vent, from something on the expressway," a teenager wrote, describing the drive home from her grandmother's wake. "But when I rolled down the windows, I just smelled diesel fumes. Grandma always loved lilacs, so I knew it was her, saying good-bye."

Touch can also be a consolation. Rudolph Freno's mother, a warm vivacious woman, had a habit of resting her hand on the right shoulder of the person she was talking to. One morning several months after her death, as Rudolph was shaving, he felt the familiar caress of his mother's hand on his right shoulder. "I looked into the mirror, but nothing was behind me," he says. He felt lovingly energized and he thanked God immediately, but he hesitated to tell anyone. Several weeks later, Rudolph visited his thoroughly pragmatic sister.

"Rudy," she began hesitantly, "remember how Mom used to rest her hand on our right shoulder when she spoke to us?"

"Yes." Rudolph knew what was coming.

"Rudy, last night I felt Mom's hand on my shoulder! I know she visited me to tell us that everything is fine."

And sometimes the touch can come through someone else. On Easter Saturday afternoon, Joan Gross of Danbury, Iowa, heard her seventeen-month-old daughter, Carol, who was napping in her crib, suddenly cry out, "Daddy! Daddy!" then settle down again. Joan assumed the baby had been dreaming. Shortly afterward, family members brought her the terrible news that her young husband had been killed in an accident.

"I wondered then if Dave had been saying good-bye to us through Carol," Joan says. She thought about it during the following months.

On Christmas morning, Joan took her children to church and sat in the pew, lonely and troubled, as services began. Two-year-old Carol was sitting next to her, absorbed with some small toys. Joan thought again of her husband, of the seemingly endless years of isolation ahead of her. If only she could sense his presence once more. . . . *Oh, Dave,* she whispered in her heart, *I sure could use a hug right now.*

Instantly little Carol stopped what she was doing. As if following an interior summons, she turned, reached out for Joan, gave her a big hug, then went back to her toys.

Tears flooded Joan in the midst of a new understanding. Life's difficulties would not go away. But neither would Dave. God would keep him right by her side, until they met again in their eternal home.

One Last
Good-Bye

*W*hen Ashley Waddle was born a few years ago, there was more than the usual family rejoicing. That was because Ashley was Mary Stutville's first great-grandchild. Not many people are privileged to have a great-grandchild, and Mary was delighted with being "Nonny" to a new generation.

Ashley's dad, Scott, is a lieutenant commander in the Navy, so he, his wife, Jill, and their little daughter moved frequently, and Mary didn't see Ashley as much as she would have liked. "But we got to Austin, Texas, where Nonny lived with Scott's parents, as often as we could, and sent photographs and letters regularly," says Jill. Nonny and Ashley occasionally talked on the phone too, building their own special bond.

The Waddles were living in Connecticut when they got the news that Nonny was in the hospital, suffering from ulcers. They were worried, but felt certain she would recover. However, her condition worsened. One night, after Scott and Jill had put Ashley to bed on the second floor, they settled down to watch television in their basement rec room. Some time later, Scott's mother called with the news that his grandmother had died.

"It's strange, but Nonny's last thoughts seemed to be of Ashley," Scott's mother told him. "During the past few days your grandmother had been talking about how sweet Ashley is, and how much she missed her." Scott hung up. Ashley wouldn't see Nonny again, not in this life, anyway.

He sat next to Jill and told her what had happened. Both were silent for a while, thinking of the woman they had loved so much. "Should we explain anything to Ashley?" Jill asked.

Scott didn't think it was necessary. Ashley wasn't even three years old and hadn't seen Nonny in several months—would she even remember her great-grandmother? And sleeping two flights above, she wouldn't have heard him on the phone.

The following morning, Ashley bounded into the bedroom and jumped on Scott and Jill's bed. "I saw Nonny!" she announced cheerfully. "She was in my room last night!"

Jill sat bolt upright. "What do you mean, Ashley?"

"Nonny came and bounced on my bed, just like this!" Ashley gave them a spirited demonstration. "She was happy. Then she said she had to go, because she was going home to heaven." Ashley bounced some more. "She's in heaven now, Mommy. Can I have breakfast?"

Scott and Jill looked at each other, awestruck. They had thought Ashley wouldn't even remember her great-grandmother. Instead, Nonny had transcended time and space to honor a special bond—and say good-bye.

Kathleen Gusloff's father-in-law died suddenly, and she and her husband were grief-stricken. It was especially hard, since their youngest child, David, was just nine months old. Now he would never know his Poppie, except through photographs and the stories Kathleen and Tom would tell him.

On the night of the funeral, the couple stayed at Tom's family home, and curled up together on a bed, with David in a playpen next to them. Tom had fallen into an exhausted sleep. Kathleen, remembering the day's sad events, was crying quietly. Suddenly she heard the baby cooing and laughing. Turning toward him in the darkened room, Kathleen saw an incredible sight. A glowing ball of light darted, flashed, and whirled in the playpen as David gurgled in pleasure.

"Oh, my God!" Kathleen leaped up and ran to the playpen. Had a fire started? She grabbed the baby's blanket to see what was in it. But again, the ball of light danced, arced around David, and then passed through him! David cooed contentedly, almost intimately, as if he *knew* something. . . . Then the light was gone. Was it an illusion?

"Tom, did you see that?" Kathleen was sure her cry had awakened her husband.

But Tom denied seeing anything. "A ball of light?" he scoffed when Kathleen tried to explain what had happened. "You must have been dreaming!"

Kathleen was hurt and confused by his attitude, and didn't know what to say.

But the next morning Tom sheepishly apologized. "I mocked your story, Kath, because I didn't want to admit that I saw what you saw," he told her. "It was a light, zigzagging around David. What could it mean?"

"For some reason, Tom, I think it was your dad," Kathleen told him slowly. "Does that sound crazy?"

"No," Tom said. He was coming to the same conclusion.

The Gusloffs never saw the light again. But several months

later, they finally put a photograph of Tom's father in their living room. David saw it and immediately toddled over. "Poppie!" he said joyfully, pointing.

How had he known?

Escort to
Paradise

*Death is simply putting out a candle because
morning has come.*

ANONYMOUS

$\mathcal{M}$arie Sullivan is the oldest of a huge extended family rooted
in Lawrence, Massachusetts. She is considered the clan historian, and she has many stories to tell.

One of the most unique happened before Marie was born.
"My parents had eleven children, but lost two as babies.
Their second child, Monica, was a perfect infant, beautiful
and healthy," says Marie. "But after her first birthday, she
became ill." The doctor could find nothing wrong, but little
Monica became weaker. "In the middle of the night on June
10, 1897, she reached up, put her hands on her mother and
father's heads, which were bent over her crib, and held them
there for a moment," says Marie. "Then she died."

At that moment, music began to play. Since this was before
the era of radio and television, Marie's father got up and went
outside on the porch, looking for the source. The Sullivans

lived a block from a Congregational church that often had evening activities. Was the music coming from there? But the neighborhood was dark and silent.

Yet, as Mr. Sullivan reentered the house, he again heard the music. It seemed somehow . . . divine. An aunt who had come to help the family during this difficult time awakened upstairs and also heard it. But she thought she must be dreaming, and she didn't tell the family until years later.

The Sullivans had several more babies, including Marie. In 1910, when Marie was eight, little Dorothy was born. But Dorothy picked up an infection at the hospital, and the doctor didn't know what to do for her. Marie and her brothers watched the baby anxiously, "but we all sensed that she was going to die," Marie says. Infant deaths were more frequent then, but always tragic.

One morning Marie awoke early, worrying about Dorothy. She lay in bed for a moment, and suddenly saw a girl in her open bedroom doorway. The girl, who appeared to be about fourteen, wore an off-white dress with wide sleeves, in the style of several years before, and her hair hung midway down her back. There was no one in Marie's house who could have matched her description. "She passed my doorway quickly, and I knew—without knowing *how* I knew—that it was my sister Monica coming to take the baby to heaven," Marie says.

"Monica! Monica!" Marie called, and leaped out of bed to follow the sister she had never seen.

"Who are you calling, dear?" her mother asked from her room.

"It's Monica, Mother. I saw her!" Marie ran through the house, searching. But she found no girl in the hallway or anywhere else.

When the children came home from school that afternoon, baby Dorothy had indeed died. Yet, instead of feeling apprehensive or frightened about her strange experience, Marie was calm, with a sense that all was well.

"I don't know why God allowed me this glimpse of Monica, but it was a very peaceful moment, despite the sorrow of losing my little sister," she says. "I felt everything was being taken care of, and all these years later, I still do."

Christmas Vision

"No eye has seen.
no ear has heard,
no mind has conceived
what God has prepared for those who love him."

1 CORINTHIANS 2:9

On Christmas Day 1960, Mary Bouillon of Fostoria, Ohio, gave birth to her first child, Karen Sue. But the next morning the doctors had grim news. Karen Sue had developed hyaline membrane disease and died during the night.

Mary and her husband were devastated. Mary's mother, Eugenia Brickner, came to her immediately. "Oh, Mom, why did this have to happen?" Mary sobbed.

"I don't know, darling, I don't know." Mary's mother rocked her, feeling helpless and frustrated. Sometimes there didn't seem to be any way to soothe the anguish.

January passed in a painful blur. "You know, Mary," Eugenia observed one afternoon, "you have your own little saint in heaven now. Imagine—Karen Sue and Jesus have the same birthday!"

"I don't want Karen Sue in heaven—I want her here!" Mary wept again. But gradually acceptance began. Mary didn't understand the *why* of it, but she had always been close to her mother, and with Eugenia's love and support, the ache in her heart became bearable.

Years passed. Mary had four healthy babies, and sometime after Mary's father died, her mother developed hardening of the arteries and entered St. Francis Home for the Aged in Tiffin, Ohio. Gradually, Eugenia's memory and speech failed, until she was only able to repeat Mary's name over and over. After a while, that stopped too. Eugenia retreated into a shell, eyes unfocused, body shrinking away from touch.

Mary was heartbroken to see her beloved mother in this condition, even sadder as Christmas approached. Memories of other Christmases flooded her, happy holidays and one especially tragic. Her mother had been an important part of them all. Now Eugenia wouldn't even be aware of the day.

On Christmas morning Mary drove to the nursing home and walked into Eugenia's room, expecting to see the familiar remote figure in the bed. But no! Her mother was looking toward the ceiling, eyes alert, with a glowing, rapturous smile on her face. As Mary watched, dumbfounded, Eugenia raised her right arm and reached toward someone.

It was as if she were communicating with familiar and beloved people. "Mom?" Mary hardly dared to ask the question. "Mom . . . are you looking at Dad and Karen Sue?"

"Sure am," Eugenia said clearly, joyfully, her eyes focused intently on a place Mary could not go. "Sure am."

Eugenia never spoke again, and she died several years later. But Mary has never forgotten that brief moment of awareness and bliss on her mother's face that Christmas morning. Surely Eugenia was attending—and still attends—the most glorious birthday party of all.

Hope's Golden Thread

It is only with the heart that one can see rightly; what is essential is invisible to the eye.

ANTOINE DE SAINT-EXUPÉRY, *THE LITTLE PRINCE*

*L*ike a golden thread from heaven, loved ones may come just when we most need encouragement. Kevin told CFRB radio listeners in Toronto about what happened when he was a shy seventeen-year-old and decided to run in his first marathon. Although Kevin's grandfather had died when Kevin was just a baby, he had always been close to his grandmother in Scotland, and before the race, he phoned her to ask for prayers. "I'll send you some special help," the elderly lady promised.

Kevin ran well, but with about two miles left, he felt himself faltering. How he hated to give up after training so hard! "Just then a youth about my age, in shorts and running shoes, overtook me," Kevin said. "I told him I was about to drop out."

"No, you can do it!" the other runner insisted. "I'll be right behind you all the way!"

Suddenly Kevin felt a surge of energy and ran on. He could

hear the youth behind him, but when he crossed the finish line and turned around, the pavement was empty.

A few days later, Kevin came across an old family album and found a yellowed photo of a young man in running shorts. His skin prickled. It was the boy who had encouraged him during the race. But how. . . ?

Kevin turned the photo over. On the back was written the young man's name. It was his grandfather, at age seventeen.

Kevin had sorely needed a boost to his self-image. Realizing that he could win if he worked hard—and that someone special was watching over him—gave him the confidence he needed to move into his adult life.

Not much was known about addiction in the 1940s when, as a farm youngster, Bob* began to drink. But by the time he was thirty-two years old, with a wife and three small children, Bob was an alcoholic. Suddenly his father died, leaving Bob to run the well-drilling business both had started several years before. "My dad missed his father very much," says daughter Chris Tuttle, "and he began to think more seriously about how he was living his own life." In April 1967, Bob completely stopped drinking.

A short time later, Bob hired a young drifter, Pete,* who was also an alcoholic. Separated from his wife, Pete had no place to stay and no transportation to and from work at the drilling well. Bob gave Pete a job, a room in his own house, and support in his attempts to stay sober. "My dad really cared a lot about helping others in need," Chris recalls. "It was not uncommon for him to lend a hand or befriend someone in Pete's position."

But despite Bob's kindness, Pete couldn't handle sobriety. He returned to alcohol, and shortly after, committed suicide.

Grief and shock over the loss of two significant people in his life, the strain of running a business, providing for his family's needs, and controlling his own addiction—it all seemed to push Bob to the brink. Gradually, his personality changed. Once lively, he became depressed, lethargic, and uncommunicative. He refused to sleep at night and paced the floor. Worried, his mother and his wife brought him to the psychiatric ward of a veterans' hospital.

But the day after Bob was hospitalized, his wife received a call from the ward. "Your husband is missing," an official told her. "He seems to have walked away."

"My mother was stunned," Chris recalls. "She told the authorities to begin a search right away." Worried friends and relatives gathered at the house. Some wept. Something terrible could happen to Bob. What should they do?

Six-year-old Chris was confused. "Why is everyone upset?" she asked.

"We can't find your father, honey," one of the relatives tried to explain.

Wasn't that what God was for? the little girl wondered. "All we have to do is tell Him about it," she pointed out.

The woman looked at Chris. Out of the mouths of babes. . . .

"You pray for your daddy," she said.

Chris climbed into bed and snuggled under the covers. She thought about her father. What did it matter if others thought him lost? God knew where he was. "God," she whispered, "I prayed for Daddy, and that's all I can do. You take care of him now. I'm tired and I'm going to sleep." And she did.

A few hours later, hospital officials found Bob. He had been wandering on a four-lane interstate highway several miles from the institution. He had no money, no telephone numbers to call, and nowhere to go for help. Furthermore, witnesses told authorities that Bob was deliberately moving to the middle of whichever lane had oncoming traffic, apparently so melancholy that being killed by a car seemed his only remaining option. But, unbelievably, nothing hit him. Always, the cars seemed to swerve just in time.

"The explanation Dad gave later convinced everyone he was hallucinating," Chris says. As a result, he was diagnosed as mentally ill and was returned to the hospital for treatment. He responded well, however, and was soon back with his family, his life restored.

But Bob and Chris attribute his cure to more than doctors and therapy. For Bob still maintains that he was not alone as he roamed the dangerous highway that night. Walking on either side of him, he says, were his father and his friend Pete, once again alive and healthy. "We've come to protect you, Bob," each of the men explained. And that's what they did, shielding him from speeding cars, banishing his lonely desolation, guarding him until help came.

Bob never saw the men again. But he believes they came that night in answer to a little girl's summons—and brought him healing and hope.

Message in the Night

*In the night of death hope sees a star, and listening
love can hear the rustle of a wing.*

ROBERT INGERSOLL, CIVIL WAR SOLDIER

"**B**ye, Ellen, see you tomorrow!" Eleanor Fisher Odom,
then sixteen years old, waved good-bye to her friend as the two
parted company on their way home from school. The girls were
part of a group who walked daily to West Division High School
in Milwaukee in the late 1920s. Ellen Harris, eligible to be
school valedictorian, was their acknowledged "princess," the
only daughter of elderly, doting parents. Everyone admired her
petite, blond beauty, but today, Eleanor thought Ellen looked
a little pale.

The next morning at school, Eleanor learned that Ellen had
been rushed to the hospital. "She had emergency surgery last
night for a burst appendix." Louise, another friend, spread
the news.

"Will she be okay?" Eleanor asked, shocked.

"Sure. We'll visit her when she's feeling better."

But Ellen did not recover. Peritonitis—a common after-surgery infection in those days—set in, then pneumonia. Ellen died a few days later.

Months passed. Mr. Harris appeared to cope with his grief and staunchly supported his wife. But Mrs. Harris was inconsolable—nothing anyone did could make her smile.

Eleanor and her friends tried to comfort the older couple by visiting them frequently. But as Mrs. Harris continued to grieve, they decided that they were not helping at all. "Maybe seeing us just reminds her of Ellen," Louise pointed out.

Eleanor sighed. "There must be a way to help her, but I don't know what it is." Confused, the girls stopped dropping by.

A year passed. Eleanor missed Ellen and wondered how Mrs. Harris was getting along. But she couldn't risk visiting the woman and adding to her sorrow. One night, Eleanor awakened abruptly, to a soft glow spreading throughout her room. As the light moved closer to her bed, it seemed to grow in size and intensity. Eleanor stared in amazement. In the middle of the warm radiance stood a lovely young girl, dressed in a flowing white gown and smiling at her. It was Ellen!

"Oh!" Was she dreaming? But no—the light was real. Eleanor reached out to grasp her friend's hand. But Ellen drew back.

"I've come with a message for you, Eleanor," she said. Although her words were serious, she seemed radiant with joy.

"For me?" Eleanor was awestruck, but—strangely—not afraid.

"Yes," the girl went on. "Thank you for being so kind to my parents. Please tell my mother I love her, and not to cry for me any longer. Tell her I'm very happy in heaven."

Before Eleanor could respond, the glow faded. She rubbed her eyes. Ellen had vanished.

Eleanor sat in stunned silence for a moment in the darkness. Why, she had been given a glimpse of heaven! Jumping out of bed, she ran to awaken her mother. "You must visit Ellen's mother and give her that message," Eleanor's mother told her.

Would Mrs. Harris believe her? Eleanor was worried, but she did as her friend had asked. "And it must have been a comfort to Mrs. Harris, because I never saw her cry again," Eleanor says today. Ellen's mother was active and productive until her death many years later—when she was reunited with the daughter who had sent her a comforting message long ago.

A White Rose, with Dew

Thus, after a season of tears, a sober and softened joy may return to us.

HENRI FREDERIC AMIEL, *JOURNAL, 21 SEPTEMBER 1868*

*T*hree-year-old Ryan James Griffin, the youngest of five children, lost his life in early June 1987. Although he was afraid of water, he was found in the family's swimming pool and died five days later. His parents, Teresa and Ray, were inconsolable. "I could barely function," Teresa says. "I felt literally crazed by grief." Why had her little son been near the pool? How had he fallen in? No one knew.

Perhaps the only thing that kept Teresa from deteriorating completely was her pregnancy. She was six months along, carrying a son already named Michael. One child can never replace another, but Teresa knew she had to stay healthy for the sake of her unborn baby.

During the days following the funeral, Teresa worried that her bond with Ryan had been broken completely. Where was he now? He was so small . . . was he safe? . . . happy? The questions tore at her. On Father's Day weekend, as she and Ray drove to the seashore for a brief getaway, Teresa was suffering intensely. "Oh, Ryan," she whispered in the car, "can you give me a sign that you're near me?"

Suddenly, into her mind came the words: "A white rose, with dew."

A white rose, with dew. What did it mean? Was it a message from Ryan? No, she must be imagining things. She was so raw with grief, so desperate to make a connection again, however fleeting. But Ryan was gone.

Later that afternoon, Teresa took a magazine down to the beach to read. She opened it at random—to a two-page ad for makeup and moisturizer—and her heart skipped a beat. In the center of the ad was a huge white rose, with dew on it.

Was it. . . ? No, surely it was just a coincidence. But later that day Ray, who did not know anything about Teresa's wish, came through the apartment door, carrying a white rose. "Here." He held it out to his wife.

"What's this for?" she asked in wonder.

"I don't know." Ray shrugged. "I saw it growing outside, and I thought I should pick it for you." Hanging from one little petal was a drop of dew.

There was much grieving still ahead, months, even years of difficulty, but Teresa was heartened from that day on by the idea that she could indeed communicate with her little boy, even if it wasn't in the same way as before. "Now, just when I need it most, a card with a white rose will arrive in the mail," she says. "Or I'll whisper to Ryan to help me with his older brother—and things somehow straighten out."

However, a year passed, then two, and Teresa was no nearer to solving the mystery: How and why did the drowning occur? She felt certain she would not heal until she knew, and she often asked God to help her find the answer.

One morning, Michael, then two and a half, came to Teresa. "Mom," he said unexpectedly, "let's talk about Ryan."

Since Michael had been born after Ryan's death, he had been told that his big brother was in heaven, but nothing more. Now he sat on the couch with Teresa and, in the direct way of children, got right to the point. "I tried to put Ryan's soul back in his body, Mom, but I couldn't," he said.

"What are you talking about, Michael?" Teresa asked, mystified. She had never heard her toddler use the word *soul*.

"He was running, and he fell and banged his head, and then he went 'glug . . . glug . . . ' " the little boy said.

Teresa's heart began to pound. "And then what, Michael?"

"Then the Light came down, like a flashlight."

"Did the Light say anything?" Tears were pricking her eyes.

"The Light said, 'I love you, Ryan.' " Michael had finished his revelation. He got off the couch and went searching for his dump truck.

But Teresa was awestruck. Michael hadn't even been born at that time—and had known nothing of the circumstances surrounding Ryan's death. And yet his description fit. If Ryan had indeed hit his head and fallen, it was the explanation she needed.

How had Michael known? But she sensed the answer to that too. Somehow her children's souls had met, one on his way to earth, the other to heaven.

Later Teresa remembered that after the funeral, the parents of one of Ryan's little playmates had told her of a similar occurrence. Their three-year-old son had insisted that Ryan had come to play with him in his room the previous night. "Ryan said he hit his head and fell into the pool," the little boy had told his parents. But no one had listened very seriously to him.

"There are many things about earthly life that we don't understand," Teresa says today. "But I think we should stay open to what God is doing, and have faith." And she has faith that she will see Ryan again. He is, she says, only a heartbeat away.[8]

BOOK FOUR

MIRACULOUS
HEALINGS

Healings from Heaven

For the Great Spirit is everywhere; he hears whatever is in our minds and hearts, and it is not necessary to speak to him in a loud voice.

BLACK ELK, PRIEST, SIOUX NATION

"*I* asked God at church to heal my stomach ulcer, but later forgot about it and kept taking my prescription. A few days later I became nauseous, and heard a voice inside me say, 'Don't you know I have healed you?' My ulcer is gone.*"

"*The Lord knew I needed a spiritual healing more than a physical one, so He changed my whole attitude about life in an overwhelming way.*"

"*Charles and Frances Hunter prayed over me for an end to my pain. A warm feeling came over me . . . I didn't need the hysterectomy!*"

"*Despite the tests, our baby was born healthy and normal.*"

"*I was delivered of all negative emotions—fear, anger,*"

hatred. The next day even my tennis partner noticed the joy in my face. 'What happened to you?' he asked."

"After my husband was diagnosed with Lou Gehrig's disease, he was given five years to live. It's been sixteen years, and he's still doing fine."

"The pain from my dislocated shoulder was intense, and there was no way I could get to a doctor. I began to pray. Within minutes, the pain left and did not return."

Judging from the letter excerpts above, many people pray for healings—and receive them in a variety of ways. Typically, medical personnel use their skills to heal us. But prayer can bring healing too. In a 1988 double-blind study at the University of California, San Francisco, cardiologists randomly divided 393 hospitalized heart patients into two groups. One was prayed for (by volunteers who did not know them), the other was not. The patients who received prayer had less complications and needed less medical intervention. In a recent Virginia poll, over 14% of adults said they had been healed either by prayer or a divine source.

Throughout history there have been people gifted with healing ministries, a special ability to pray over the sick, just as Jesus' apostles did. (Such people have no power of their own—if a healing takes place, it always comes from God.) In other instances, illnesses vanish, emotional peace descends, without anyone else being involved. "Today more than ever, physicians are cooperating with patients to make office records and X rays available for review and study by legitimate investigators," says Harald Bredesen, pastor and author of *Need a Miracle?* "So a great deal more hard evidence now exists to prove that many claimed miracles are real miracles."

God wants his children to be well, and He may heal a person

instantly. But often, healing happens over a long period of time, and sometimes it doesn't happen at all. Why?

We must never make the mistake of blaming ourselves or the invalid, for only God knows the answer to the ultimate mysteries of life and death. It's possible, though, that a few of us may impede our own healing. Medical evidence exists to show that anger, vengefulness, and other negative emotions can sometimes block recovery. As the African proverb reminds us, "He who forgives ends the quarrel . . ." and takes a giant step on the road to physical and emotional health.

Healing may also be delayed because God is using difficulties in our lives to develop our spiritual muscles, to lift us to levels of understanding, compassion, wisdom that we might not otherwise reach. What is initially considered a hardship might well turn out to be His invitation to grace and growth, even a way to help others later. "The best doctors are often those who've been seriously ill themselves," observes Dr. Bernie Siegel, author of *Love, Medicine & Miracles*. Only a cancer patient can truly understand the unique suffering of another in identical circumstances—and offer just the right mixture of comfort and care.

"The Koran teaches that God does not send sickness," explains Dr. Musa Qutub, president of the Islamic Information Center of America. "But sickness can wash away bad deeds; it can change us. Adversity is a profound teacher." We should rejoice and give thanks when difficulties occur, not because of the suffering itself, but because of what will come of it, if we lean on God.

For example, Mark needed back surgery, and he asked a minister to pray over him for healing. The minister did, but nothing changed. Mark went through a painful operation, and gradually the men lost touch.

Two years later, Mark rang the minister's doorbell. "We're

moving out of town," he explained, "and I wanted to thank you for the healing you helped bring about."

"I?" The minister was bewildered. "But, Mark, you weren't healed."

Mark smiled. "Yes I was, Reverend. You didn't know it, but at the time you prayed for me, my personal life was a mess. My wife had sued for divorce, one son was on drugs, and our daughter was estranged from the family."

Because Mark was suffering, however, everyone dutifully rallied around his bedside. Gradually, during his long convalescence, family members began to talk to one another in ways they'd previously been too busy, too angry to do. Slowly, attitudes changed, hearts mended. "My family has reconciled, Reverend," Mark finished. "And it wouldn't have happened except for my surgery. God gave me the healing I *needed,* instead of the one I thought I wanted."

In other cases, God simply says "not yet." "We live in an age of instant tea, instant photos," says Sister Briege McKenna, who has an international healing ministry. "And we treat God the same. We think that if God doesn't give us what we want right away, then He isn't giving it to us at all."

A couple brought their little boy to Sister Briege. His inoperable brain tumor would soon cause blindness, then death. "I can pray with you," Sister said, "but you and your family must also pray for David's healing."

"Sister," said the father, "we're not too good at praying."

"Just talk," Sister explained. "Lay hands on David and bless him."

The couple went home, gathered their older children, and decided to pray together for David each night after supper. Time passed, and the tumor got bigger. David's father became discouraged, but his mother insisted they continue. At the end of seven months, everyone realized that although the tumor was still growing, David had not gone blind. Prayertime continued.

After about sixteen months, the growth started to shrink and gradually disappeared. "Then I realized that during those two years, our children had been transformed," David's father said. Even after David recovered, his siblings refused to leave the house after supper until everyone prayed together. Had David's healing been instant, the family would never have experienced this wonderful gift.[9]

It's important to remember, as you read these stories, that documented healings such as these are rare. Though beautiful and moving, these stories are not intended to dissuade anyone from first and foremost seeking help from trained and licensed medical practitioners—and then following through with the recommended treatment. On the contrary, as in all things in life, God expects us to do our part when it comes to our health. He wants us to take good care of ourselves at all times, which means seeking proper medical care when we fall ill. Also, He wants us to heed the warnings of clergy of all religions to beware of charlatans who masquerade as "healers" and prey on the ill and the weak in order to enrich themselves. Such con artists, motivated not by love of God and a desire to help others, but by greed and selfishness, should be shunned.

When we are ill, of course we should pray. But we must always keep in mind that prayer isn't a magic formula for good health. Sometimes, no matter how sincerely we pray, how diligently we cooperate with physicians, however good and kind and blameless we are, recovery does not happen. At such times we must walk in faith, with prayer itself as a blessing, a way of bringing peace to ourselves and those around us. God's reasons may not be immediately apparent, but we can always be sure that He knows what He's doing—and will never abandon us.

The True
Thanksgiving

And though I weep because those sails are tattered,
Still will I cry, while my best hopes lie shattered,
"I trust in Thee!"

ELLA WHEELER WILCOX

$\mathcal{I}$t was Thanksgiving 1988. Jane and Alban Theriault's children and grandchildren were at their house in Lewiston, Maine, to celebrate—in both French and English (the family has always been bilingual). Alban lifted the huge turkey out of the oven, set it on the countertop, and loaded the baster with drippings for a final squirt.

Just then, the Theriaults' nine-year-old granddaughter, Kari, skipped up. "Pepere, can I help?" she asked.

"Be careful, dear," Alban began, but to his horror, the boiling-hot fat spurted out of the dropper in his hand and splashed over Kari's face. "Oh no!" he shouted as the little girl screamed in pain. People came running from every room.

Kari was badly burned. Gravy drippings had splattered on her chin and half of her mouth, and had scalded her tongue.

Liquid had also fallen on her chest, and since her dress was made of nylon, the high heat had burned even more deeply.

Kari's mother, Christine, a nurse, decided not to take her hysterical daughter to the hospital. She did everything for Kari that the emergency-room staff would have done, then put her in Alban and Jane's bed.

"Kari cried for four hours," Jane recalls. "Her skin split open and hung from her chin. The blotches on her chest were raw. It was the worst Thanksgiving any of us had ever had."

Perhaps Alban was the most devastated. How had he allowed this to happen? Kari would be scarred for life—and every time she looked in the mirror, she would blame her grandfather. It was almost more than this quiet, gentle man could bear.

On Friday and Saturday, Kari's pain increased. Her tongue was badly burned, and her lips stuck together. Liquids from a straw were her only nourishment. Her face got worse and worse. Jane and Alban had four tickets for Father Ralph DiOrio's healing service on Sunday in Worcester. "Why don't we take Kari so Father can pray over her?" Jane suggested. Christine agreed.

There are usually thousands of people at this kind of service, and crowd control is imperative. "No one can get to Father DiOrio unless *he* calls *you*," Jane explains. But Jane couldn't wait for that. When the priest left the stage to bless people in the balcony, Jane grasped Kari's hand, went to the opposite end of the hall, outside and around the building, then inside, right where he was approaching.

An usher came up, presumably to tell Jane she was blocking the aisle and would have to leave. "But I could hear Father making his way through the crowds, and as he came down some stairs, I turned Kari around toward him," she recalls.

Father DiOrio stopped. "What happened to her?" he asked Jane.

"She's been burned with hot gravy, Father."

The priest took holy oil from his pocket, touched Kari's wounds with it, and prayed for her healing. Jane began to thank God. She felt certain that everything would be all right.

The next morning when Kari awakened, she said, "I'm hungry, Mom. Can I have some real food?"

Christine looked at her. Her raw face and chest didn't seem any better. "Kari, you know you can't eat," she reminded her.

"Mom, I'm fine. Nothing hurts, really."

Kari did eat an enormous breakfast, so Christine agreed to send her to school. Kari's teacher and classmates were horrified at her injuries, and she spent all day explaining what had happened. But on Tuesday, oddly, the wounds seemed to be closing. On Thursday when Kari got up, her mother screamed. "Kari! Look in the mirror!"

Kari did. Neither of them could believe what they saw. Kari's skin was smooth and perfect. Not a scar, not even a blister remained to show where the sores had been. Her teacher and friends were astonished too. How could such terrible wounds simply vanish?

Alban Theriault took Kari with him to prayer meeting that week. He held her high in his arms, tears of joy spilling down his cheeks, his broken heart mended. And Jane, too, pondered this wonderful occurrence. "It was interesting that we just 'happened' to have four tickets for the healing service," she muses. "And even more interesting that God took away Kari's pain first, but not her burns—which allowed her to go to school, where many witnessed the damage."

Days later, everyone saw a little girl's perfectly restored face— and knew what God had done.

Double Blessings

There are no mistakes, no coincidences. All events are blessings given to us to learn from.

DR. ELISABETH KÜBLER-ROSS, PSYCHIATRIST AND AUTHOR

*L*ike many men of his generation, Richard Slade volunteered for duty in Vietnam during the height of the conflict. He flew both attack and Medvac helicopters during two tours of duty, but escaped being wounded. When he finally came home, his family heaved a collective sigh of relief and thanksgiving. Rick's troubles were over.

In fact, they were just beginning. But it would be many years before the impact of the chemical Agent Orange was fully understood. In the meantime, Rick married, started a family, taught flight mechanics, and enlisted in the National Guard. In the summer of 1991, the Guard offered him a full-time job in Germany as a test pilot at a helicopter-repair facility. It was the job of his dreams.

"Before Rick and his wife, Shirley, left for Germany, he did complain about stomach pains," his sister, Pam Wallen, recalls. "He thought he was developing an ulcer. But he had just had a flight physical, and nothing showed up."

Rick hadn't been in Germany for more than a few weeks, however, when one morning he doubled over in pain. "Something's exploded in my stomach!" he cried to a friend, who rushed him to the hospital. Within hours, he was in surgery. Doctors didn't find a perforated ulcer, however. It was cancer, invading Rick's stomach, liver, and colon. Later, doctors discovered that it was also in his bone marrow.

The surgeon removed ninety percent of Rick's stomach in an attempt to keep him alive long enough to undergo chemotherapy. But he was honest with Rick. Vietnam hadn't killed Rick, not directly. But the long-term effects of chemical warfare had finally caught up with him. There was no cure for this kind of cancer. Rick's condition was terminal.

Pam was devastated at the news. Her mother-in-law had just died of cancer, and now her beloved brother had it. Pam had always believed in the power of prayer, but "I'd never received a big miracle," she says. In fact, it was hard to imagine that kind of thing happening to ordinary people like her, like Rick. When Pam prayed for anyone with cancer, she now added a prayer for her brother. But when Rick came back to Sam Houston Hospital in San Antonio to start his treatments, her sense of despair deepened.

Then Pam was invited to a Sunday-night prayer service for her friend Carol. Doctors had found a tumor that was probably malignant, and Carol was going in for surgery the following day. "Carol was my first Bible teacher and really taught me to pray," Pam explains. "I didn't expect a miracle, not really, but I wanted to support her. So I went."

Pam found the service very moving. More than a hundred friends and family members had come. Carol sat in a chair, holding her baby grandson, while people stood in a loving circle around her. They sang, read from Scripture, praised and thanked God for whatever good He would bring out of this situation, laid hands on Carol, and anointed her with oil. Pam felt tears pricking her eyes during this ancient and grace-filled ritual. This was what the Bible *told* us to do when illness struck, she realized. Down through the ages her spiritual sisters and brothers had done this very thing, and healing had come. Why then, and not now?

God, Pam said silently, *I've been praying, but tonight I'm going to ask You for more, for miracles. I'm asking for one for Carol because that's why I came. But I'm sneaking in an extra request for Rick.* With God, there was no time or space, she knew. If He could heal Carol here, He could certainly heal a man in an oncology ward in Texas.

On Monday word spread through the neighborhood quickly, joyfully. Carol's doctor had had a surprise. Carol's tumor was not only benign but somehow it also had turned out to be so small that it didn't require surgery after all. "We were thrilled, and I remember thinking—we got our miracle!" Pam says. "I kind of forgot about Rick." After all, people didn't get *two* miracles, did they?

But Tuesday night Rick phoned. It had been at least a month since he and Pam had talked, but when Pam heard his voice, her heart almost stopped. "I have some news for you," Rick said slowly.

God, could it be. . . ? She knew, but was afraid to speak.

"Pam, I'm in complete remission. There's nothing . . . nothing. They even took bone marrow out of my hip. All of a sudden there's no sign of cancer! And today a CAT scan came back clean. The doctors can't believe it."

"Rick, I went to a healing service on Sunday, and I asked for a miracle for you. . . ." Any minute now she would weep with the wonder of it.

There was a thoughtful silence on the other end of the phone. "So did Shirley's aunt," Rick said finally. "Pam, I think I'm healed."

A few years have passed since that exquisite night. Rick, who was told not to lift anything heavier than a piece of paper because of surgical aftereffects, is now restoring his 1949 Ford pickup and enjoying wrestling with his baby grandson. And Pam? She has learned to *ask* and to expect great things from God. And she's quick to tell people why.[10]

Miracle from Michael

He has His reasons for doing what He does, and He will explain them to us someday.

EMIDIO JOHN PEPE, A READER FROM ASTORIA, NEW YORK

*I*n 1956, Catherine Webb began a battle with cancer. First, a hysterectomy, next a double mastectomy, followed by several skin cancers. It was traumatic, and "without my wonderful surgeon, I doubt I would have come through as well as I did," Catherine says. In 1983, however, her doctor died.

A year later, Catherine noticed new symptoms, and her current physicians put her in the hospital for tests. Eventually, all three came to her bedside, their faces grim. Catherine now had cancer in her colon and liver. They recommended surgery, followed by chemotherapy and radiation.

Catherine refused. "There comes a time when you just have to say, 'enough,'" she told the doctors.

All of them were angry at her stubbornness. "What are you going to do?" one demanded. "How will you deal with this?"

It was a good question. Catherine hadn't thought that far

ahead—she was still reeling from the shock of this devastating and final diagnosis—but she took a deep breath. "If it's spread to my liver, then there's really nothing more that can be done, medically," she said quietly. "But I have a deep faith in God. And that, plus living my life one day at a time—and keeping my sense of humor—ought to get me through whatever is waiting."

The second doctor shook his head. "You'll have less than a year—maybe only six months," he told her.

"All the more reason *not* to go through these treatments," Catherine replied. Already she was thinking about alternatives. Perhaps hospice nurses could help her through her remaining days.

Catherine went home from the hospital sick, in pain, and very weak. "My nurses were wonderful," she says, "but they had to do almost everything for me." Her energy faded and her world shrank to the distance between a chair in her living room and her bed. Sometime between December 1984 and June 1985, she would die. She prayed to face it with courage.

One morning several weeks after her diagnosis, Catherine's nurse brought her the mail. As the nurse opened one letter for her, something dropped out. "Look at this," she said, giving the items to Catherine.

There was a leaflet and a small gold medal of Saint Michael of the Saints. Catherine had never heard of him. But the leaflet said that he was the patron saint of cancer patients and that the prayers printed on the little paper were to be said in the hope of a cure for cancer.

Who had sent this to her? Her address was typewritten rather than computerized, and the envelope bore the return address of a Father Anthony at a Baltimore monastery. There was no letter inside. Catherine had never heard of Father Anthony, either, but obviously he had heard of her. Or perhaps a friend had sent her name to him.

It was, of course, too late for Catherine, but the idea of asking a special saint to intercede for *other* cancer patients appealed to her. During the next few weeks, she thought about Saint Michael, and prayed for sick people everywhere whenever she could.

One morning Catherine awakened early. She felt strange, as if energy were running through her. Although she hadn't walked alone in weeks, she got up and made her shaky way to the bathroom. By the time the nurses arrived, she was back in bed.

"Don't bother." She waved one cheerfully away. "I've already been to the bathroom."

"Stop teasing," the nurse said, smiling.

"Check the light," Catherine told her. "I knew you wouldn't believe me, so I left it on."

Both nurses went to the bathroom. The light was on. "How did you do that?" one asked in amazement.

Catherine laughed. "I honestly don't know."

The next day, Catherine felt even stronger. Gradually, her symptoms disappeared and she took on a greater part of her own care. Had she been healed? When her physician examined her a few weeks later, Catherine got an even greater surprise.

"There's been no change," the doctor told her. "All the tumors are still there. But . . . they seem to have stopped growing."

"Then I'm in remission?"

The doctor didn't answer. He knew—and Catherine knew—that in her case, "remission" was impossible. But Catherine felt fine. In fact, she soon dismissed her hospice nurses.

Today, nine years later, Catherine leads an active life. Scans still show cancer throughout her liver and colon, but she takes no medicine or treatments. She gets four or five "bad spells" a year, she says, "so I go to bed, pray till it eases, get up, and go on." The rest of the time she visits cancer patients and spreads the word about Saint Michael of the Saints. "People come to me in the most unexpected ways, and I hear later of many cures and remissions. Even those who die do so with enormous peace. I don't know why God has gotten me into this, but I'm grateful to do it for Him."

And Catherine is grateful for something else too. After she realized what had happened to her, she sent her medical records and a letter of thanks to Father Anthony in Baltimore. "I am so glad you mailed me the leaflet and medal," she wrote him. "As you can see, I have certainly made good use of them!"

Father Anthony wrote back, rejoicing at Catherine's news. "However," he added, "I think you should know that we have never heard of you, you are not on our mailing list, we have no record of sending you anything nor did anyone request that we do so. God works in mysterious ways, doesn't He?"

Catherine certainly agrees.[11]

A Forgiving Heart

Should a man nourish anger against his fellows
And expect healing from the Lord?

SIRACH 28:3

$\mathcal{P}$eople call Paul Musielak the "Miracle Man," because he has received not only one miraculous healing, but two. In July 1981, Paul, a normal, healthy twenty-one-year-old, developed some strange symptoms. He was slightly ill when his physician sent him to Houston's Northwest Medical Center for tests. But a few days later, Paul was paralyzed and had gone blind. "We think your son has spinal meningitis," the doctors told Paul's shocked parents. Despite treatment, however, Paul's condition remained the same, and eventually this diagnosis was ruled out. Baffled physicians sent him to Sharpstown General Hospital to see a noted neuro-ophthalmologist.

"Each day Paul's mom or I or whoever was visiting him would pray together for his healing," says Paul's father, Richard. But nothing happened. Paul remained unable to see or move. Finally Richard called a priest friend, and one evening when just the two men were in the room, they prayed over Paul.

Paul is vague about that night. But he does remember the priest.

"He told me to picture Jesus in my mind," Paul says. "And I did. The next thing I knew, I was going through a tunnel, like a kaleidoscope of color, beautiful and bright and light. . . . And at the end, I saw Jesus."

Although conscious, Paul lapsed into a profound peace. A short time later, as his father carried him to the bathroom, he realized that he was feeling better. Two days later, he left the hospital with no sign of paralysis, and his vision rapidly returned to normal.

His family never discovered what strange malady had made Paul so sick, but everyone was thrilled and grateful at his recovery. That, however, was to be only his first miracle.

Some two years later, Paul pulled into a convenience-store parking lot one Friday night, got out of his car, and was suddenly hit in the face with a club—not once, but several times. Apparently he had stepped into a fight between some young men, and without provocation, they beat him unmercifully. "Let's get out of here!" one of them said as Paul fell to the ground. It was the last thing he remembered.

Richard Musielak was in bed when he received a phone call from the police. "Your son is in the hospital," someone told him. "You had better come."

Richard raced to the hospital, and stopped in shock at the door of his son's room, hardly able to look at his terribly injured face. "Paul's eyes were out to here, swollen and bleeding, and no one knew yet if his vision would be permanently damaged," Richard says. "He had multiple contusions. X rays showed a skull fracture and a possible fractured nose and orbital bone. The doctors suspected brain damage. He was a mess."

"Paul, who did this to you?" Richard asked, horrified, almost afraid to touch the bloodied body in the bed. But Paul could give him no information, and neither could the police. Witnesses had assumed Paul was part of the fighting, and no one really knew what had happened.

Aghast and frustrated, Richard left for home. And as he drove, a white-hot rage began to build. He would get them. He would find the punks who had done this to his beloved son, and he would. . . . Images of himself buying a baseball bat, tracking them down, breaking their kneecaps before turning them over to the authorities made his heart race. His wife was distraught, so when he reached home, he soothed her as best he could. Then he lay sleepless for the rest of the night.

By dawn, Richard's plans had taken shape. He would start by putting Wanted posters up on poles near where the crime had occurred. Then he would walk the streets, paying for any tips he could glean from those who knew these things. Through the day his rage escalated, especially that afternoon when he visited Paul again. His son was just the same. Doctors had nothing encouraging to report.

Paul's mother and brothers and sisters were devastated. Some visited Paul and prayed. Richard didn't have time for prayer. He was on another kind of mission.

The next morning, Sunday, Richard went to mass alone, but paid scant attention to the altar. His mind was still focused on the job ahead. Find the thugs. Beat them. Pay them back for what they had done to Paul. . . .

Slowly Richard realized that the priest was preaching the homily. Ironically, it was on the theme of forgiveness. *Not today,* Richard almost said out loud. That was the last thing he needed to hear.

But the message encircled him, pierced him right down to his soul. The priest was preaching on Matthew 5:23–24:

". . . [I]f you are offering your gift at the altar and there remember that your brother has something against you, leave your gift there in front of the altar. First go and be reconciled to your brother; then come and offer your gift." The words were familiar. Richard had heard them since he was a child, and he had always thought he understood and obeyed them. But this, this was different.

Surely God did not mean *him*. Not now, in this situation! He could *not* absolve those men—they deserved to be punished! And yet . . . didn't he know that an unforgiving heart could block healing? He did need to be healed of his anger, to abandon his plan for vengeance. Ultimately, no good could really come of it. How would it help Paul or his wife or family if he, Richard, was arrested for assault? But how could he let go?

He bowed his head. *God, help me,* he prayed. *I don't feel like forgiving, I don't want to forgive. But if You're asking me to do it, I will. . . .* He would not *forget,* he knew. Forgiveness didn't work like that. It was an act of the will, not the emotions. Instead, he would remember, live with the feelings, the memory, the scars on his son's face, and forgive anyway.

Richard felt no better when he came out of church and headed for the hospital to visit Paul. When he stepped off the hospital elevator, however, a nurse was waiting for him. "Mr. Musielak, we don't know how to explain it," she began.

"Explain what?"

"It's Paul. He—"

"Paul!" Had he taken a turn for the worse? Richard raced down the hall into the room—and stopped in his tracks.

Paul was sitting up in bed, his face almost perfect. No contusions, not even a scab marred his features. His eyes were the proper size, just slightly bloodshot, with no bruises or swelling to be seen. "The skull fracture isn't showing up on the X ray," another nurse told him. "He seems to be fine."

Richard thought of the bloodied mess he'd seen yesterday. "How could this be?" he asked, incredulous.

The nurse just shook her head.

Paul went home on Monday, since the doctors could find no reason to confine an obviously healthy young man, and he is healthy to this day. His dad is too—physically, emotionally, and most of all, spiritually. Making a conscious decision to forgive was perhaps the most difficult and seemingly useless step Richard had ever taken. But the Teacher within him honored his sacrifice—and gave him a gift he would treasure for the rest of his life.

Helping Hands

> ... *[Y]et none of them received what had been*
> *promised. God had planned something better* ...
>
> Hebrews 11:39–40

Wilma Phillips has had diabetes since she was twenty-three. Despite several serious episodes, she has always felt protected.

One morning Wilma waved her nine- and eight-year-olds off on the school bus, put her newborn son, Robby, in his crib and nineteen-month-old Susan in the playpen. Ah! Some quiettime to write a letter. Wilma sat at the kitchen table, but by nine-thirty she was seeing double and feeling sweaty and dizzy. Wilma knew she was having an unexpected—and dangerous—insulin reaction, and she needed a drink of orange juice or something to eat in order to raise her blood-sugar level. Her father-in-law, a physician, had often reminded her that this situation could lead to a coma—and a coma could lead to death. But she was alone with the babies, already too weak to get to the refrigerator. And it would feel so nice just to slip into sleep. . . .

"Suddenly, I felt a hand grip my right shoulder and shake

me so hard and fast that I sat up," she says. Had her husband, Robert, come home unexpectedly? But there was no one in the kitchen. After a few moments, she slumped over again. And again, the hand shook her awake!

The pattern continued. Wilma kept lapsing into unconsciousness, kept being jounced and pushed by the unseen guardian. As if from a great distance, she occasionally heard Susan fussing in the playpen, hungry because she was missing her lunch. But after a while the toddler quieted. Robby slept the entire time, despite not being fed or changed.

Hours passed. At four-fifteen, her older children returned. Wilma was still sitting, still conscious. "Mom!" one shouted in dismay. The other ran for orange juice.

Instead of being in a coma or brain-dead, Wilma was fine, although her father-in-law believes such a recovery would have been impossible. And why hadn't the babies cried? "I'm sure God sent angels all around the house that day," Wilma says.

A few years later, the family drove from their farm in Iowa toward the Wisconsin Dells for a long weekend of fun. They stayed Friday night in a small town. The next morning Wilma got ready to take her insulin, and couldn't find it. "I remembered my supply bag sitting on the dining-room table at home," she says. Had she left it there?

"We'll find a drugstore and get what you need," Robert assured her.

It was early Saturday morning, however, and nothing was open. The family drove on, and the car began to make funny noises. What if they broke down on this rural road? And what would happen to Wilma if she didn't find insulin soon?

Just then Wilma heard a clear voice: "I will supply all your needs in Reedsburg," it said.

"Did you hear that?" she asked Robert.

"Hear what?"

Wilma didn't know what to say. Was her lack of insulin causing hallucinations? And where was Reedsburg?

They were coming upon a town. "Maybe there'll be something open here," Robert said.

"No," Wilma heard herself answer. "This isn't Reedsburg."

"Wilma, what are you talking about?" Robert asked, by now a bit exasperated.

But Wilma was right. Everything was closed, and Robert drove on. The car was still making funny noises, the children were hungry, and Wilma was still apprehensive. Just then, they passed a sign. Reedsburg!

Ahead was a gas station, open for business. They pulled in, and the attendant looked at the car. It was a minor problem, and while the attendant fixed it, Robert explained that Wilma was a diabetic without insulin. "Our drugstore isn't open yet," the attendant explained, "but you could probably get a shot at the hospital." He gave them directions, and Robert pulled away quickly. But a mile or two later, he realized they were lost.

By now, Wilma was worried. The children had looked forward to this trip, and she didn't want to ruin their fun. *God,* she prayed silently, *if that was You I heard, please help. . . .*

Just then a car came by. "Do you know where the hospital is?" Robert called to the driver.

"Someone sick?" the woman called back.

"My wife needs insulin—" Robert began, but the driver stopped him.

"Pull over," she said. "I'm a diabetic, and I have everything at home that she needs."

She turned around quickly, drove away and was back moments later with the right brand of insulin, as well as a disposable needle and alcohol pads. Within minutes Wilma was feeling fine. The family found a restaurant, then a drugstore for more insulin, then drove on to find accommodations that night near the Dells.

But everything was too expensive. Wilma remembered the words she had heard. "Let's drive back to Reedsburg," she suggested. They did, and found a large affordable room.

Finally! The family put their bags in the room and got ready to leave for the Dells. "Wait—I need something from my suitcase," Wilma told Robert. She opened it, and there was her missing supply bag. "I know it wasn't there earlier when I looked," she said. But God had promised to provide *all* their needs, and so He had, in His own way.

Wilma's Assembly of God congregation often prays for healings for people. Yet Wilma has not been healed of diabetes. Does she wonder why? "I know that God wants us to be physically healthy," she says, "but sometimes there are other things He also wants for us. I think my condition has caused me to draw very close to Him, to depend on Him for everything. This brings me peace and freedom from worry—and maybe that's the best healing of all."

Vision on
the Windshield

What's a miracle, Andy?
God.
That's all?
God payin' attention to you.

SANDRA PRATT MARTIN,
BITE YOUR TONGUES

On a bright fall day in the 1970s, twelve-year-old Anne Tichenor came home grinning. "We were riding bikes, and some boys threw crab apples at us," she announced to her mother, Cynthia Goldsberry. "I got hit in the eye."

Cynthia hid a smile. Flirting rituals had changed a bit since *she* had attended school, but there was no doubt her daughter had enjoyed the encounter! Anne's left eye looked and felt fine, so there seemed to be no damage done.

Cynthia was on the phone a few hours later, when she heard Anne scream in terror. "Mom! Mom!" Not only was Anne now feeling intense pain in her eye, she could no longer see.

Cynthia rushed her to the ophthalmologist. The news was not good. Anne's eye was hemorrhaging from the blow, a condition called traumatic hyphema, which can cause permanent damage to vision. Treatment at that time consisted of patching both eyes and having a patient lie quietly for five days, with the head of the bed slightly elevated so that there would not be fresh hemorrhaging as the blood clot dissolved.

"I can call an ambulance, or you can drive Anne to the hospital," the doctor told Cynthia. "But it's important that she not be jolted at all." He bandaged both her eyes, and Cynthia put her in the car.

Cynthia will never forget the drive to the hospital. "I was dazed at the unexpected and terrible thing that had just happened to us," she says. "I took side streets and drove about ten miles an hour, all the while trying to grasp the fact that Anne might lose her vision."

Anne had absorbed the same message. Along the way, she asked her mother to describe the red and yellow autumn leaves, the birds, even the clouds in the sky, as if she might never see them again.

At the hospital, the staff whisked Anne off, and Cynthia attempted to phone her husband, who was out of the country on business. No luck. When she saw Anne again, her daughter was lying in bed, both eyes patched. "Vaguely, I noticed her hair—the nurses had arranged it by fanning it out above her head on the pillow," Cynthia says. "Anne never lay in bed with her hair up like that." But it was late, and Cynthia had to get back to her other children. She kissed her daughter gently and went home. Only then did she let the tears come.

Early the following morning, before they left for work, Cynthia called two close friends in her United Methodist congregation and asked them to pray and spread the word. Both were shocked and saddened, since they knew all of Cynthia's children, and were very fond of them.

"It's a tragedy," Norma* told her husband, Jim,* as both

of them left the house. "Anne's vision could be seriously damaged."

Jim thought about Anne all day. What a terrible thing. But what could he do to help? He considered himself a believer in Jesus, but he had never prayed specifically for anything, especially not for a healing. He wouldn't know how.

But did it really take any special knowledge? There was that child, God's child, in the hospital. And here *he* was, willing to do anything. Driving home that evening, Jim took a deep breath. "Jesus," he heard himself saying aloud in the car, "Anne doesn't need this problem. Please take care of it right away."

Jim had been approaching a Stop sign. Now as he slowed the car, it was as if a curtain came down on the inside of his windshield, almost like a wide television screen. On it he could see a scene of some kind. It was a hospital room, with someone in a bed. . . . Why, it was Anne! He could see her clearly, both her eyes bandaged. And her hair—he had never seen it like that, fanned out above her on the pillow.

But Anne wasn't alone. Standing next to her at the head of the bed, visible only from about the chest down, was the glowing figure of a tall man. Was it a doctor? No. This man was wearing a white robe.

Astonished, Jim watched as the man's hand came down and gently cupped Anne's left eye. It was a healing gesture—Jim knew it without being told—and he realized that his prayer was being answered. Gradually the tableau faded, and the Stop sign again came into view.

Shaken, Jim drove home and phoned Cindy. "Are *both* Anne's eyes bandaged?" he asked abruptly.

"Yes. But how did you know?"

"Which one did she injure?"

"The left," Cindy answered. "Why?"

But Jim couldn't talk about it, not until he had had time to think—and wonder.

After five days, Cindy took Anne, still bandaged, to the ophthalmologist. "I had been at peace ever since Jim told me about what he'd seen," Cynthia says. "But Anne was in with the doctor so long that I began to get apprehensive again."

Finally, the doctor came into the waiting room. "This is wonderful!" he told Cynthia. "I expected Anne to lose at least thirty percent of her vision, perhaps more, due to the damage. But both her eyes are perfect. It's as if nothing ever happened."

Everyone knows, however, that something did happen, something wonderful. God came.

Circle of Love

> Remember the Father's dream and the care He took
> to craft a world for His children. But most of all,
> remember that each time you praise Him, each time
> your heart goes out to someone else, you're reflecting
> His light.
>
> MAX LUCADO, THE CHRISTIAN READER,
> SEPTEMBER/OCTOBER 1992

*I*t was in November of 1991 that Dianne Mistelske noticed symptoms of malaria. She wasn't particularly worried, just concerned that her busy pace as wife, mother, and worker for Habitat for Humanity would be temporarily interrupted. "Having had malaria often when I was a lay missionary in Tanzania, I knew that you begin to feel better soon after the treatment starts," she says. So she went to the hospital for five days, and was then sent home, supposedly on the mend.

"Home," however, was not the usual American city or suburb, the ordinary American life, but instead, Botswana, Africa. Dianne had worked for a mission organization in Minneapolis after college, and she had met her future husband there. "John eventually joined the Peace Corps and went to Botswana for two years," Dianne says. "When he came back, we got married and decided to go overseas together." The couple was sent back to Africa, just for another two years.

"But there is a saying here that once you are pricked with a thorn in Africa, you get Africa in your blood," Dianne says with a smile. She didn't know that her brief Peace Corps stint would turn into a lifetime commitment.

It did—but not until after the Mistelskes had finished their hitch and returned to teach at a mission school in New Mexico. However, they missed Africa so much that they went back on several assignments, eventually settling in Botswana as project directors for Habitat for Humanity, a worldwide philanthropic organization based in Georgia that provides housing for needy people.

They also—between 1984 and 1988—went from a family of two to seven. "Having been told that I probably would not conceive, we were blessed with the chance to adopt two African children," Dianne says. Shortly afterward, Dianne became pregnant—twice! Eventually a third adopted child rounded out their home.

So it was a busy and full life that Dianne expected to resume as soon as she recovered from malaria. Her accounting chores as well as her work with families selected to be Habitat homeowners was already far behind schedule and she was anxious to catch up. But one week stretched into two, then three. Dianne felt weaker each day, and one morning her complexion turned an unhealthy yellow. Malaria had led to acute hepatitis.

Three more weeks in the hospital were followed by two months at home. She tried to rally, but she was still completely exhausted and had pain in her liver area. "Many people who'd had hepatitis assured me that recovery could be slow," Dianne says, "and I pushed myself to keep up with the responsibilities of family, home, and work." But each day she felt she was climbing a mountain. The aches and fatigue continued.

Dianne's doctor returned to the United States in July and August, so Dianne skipped the usual liver-function tests. But she felt as though she were moving backward, and "it became harder and harder to do anything at all." Finally, in September, she went to a specialist.

"You'll need to go to Johannesburg for further tests," the specialist said.

"Am I in trouble?" Dianne asked.

"Your condition could be caused by chronic hepatitis, or tumors, or cancer or secondary problems from rheumatoid arthritis," he said gently. "But, yes. You have liver dysfunction. And that's very serious."

Dianne and John have always believed in the power of prayer. And now they put it to the test. Phone calls to their family and friends, their church community, and the Habitat for Humanity staff in the United States came first. "Pray," the word went out across the world, to all the people in all the little towns where the Mistelskes had worked and served others. "Storm heaven. Now it's our turn to help Dianne."

Next came their neighbors. Muslims and Hindus, some teachers, some volunteers on Habitat projects. The social worker who had found their adopted daughter. The shop-keepers who greeted them warmly each day, the local children. As they prepared for Johannesburg, John and Dianne felt love surrounding them, buoying and filling them with courage. They could handle whatever came, they knew. God and His people were with them.

For a week in Johannesburg, Dianne went through every imaginable test. But there was nothing wrong with her. Nothing at all.

"Your liver is completely normal," the physician finally told her.

"How could this be?" she asked, tears streaming down her face.

He shrugged. "I have no explanation."

"I know God has healed me for a reason, and I pray I can discern how best to follow Him and love Him," says Dianne, busy in Botswana and now in vibrant health. "And I'm totally overwhelmed when I realize how many beautiful people shared in this miracle."

For that is a miracle too. A less noticeable one, perhaps, but important just the same. Because, for a little while, prayer mats rolled out, incense burned, drumbeats and chants ascended; some people petitioned God in yarmulkes and prayer shawls, some read the Bible, some recited the rosary, some lit votive candles and held hands. All colors. All faiths. And because of Dianne, all united.

Perhaps it is just the beginning of what could be. . . .

BOOK FIVE

GOD'S
SPECIAL
MIRACLES

The Measure
of God's Love

I sing the mighty power of God
That makes the mountains rise,
That spread the flowing seas abroad
And built the lofty skies . . .

ISAAC WATTS,
"I SING THE MIGHTY POWER OF GOD"

"*I* was driving home from visiting my daughter in the hospital in Sparta, New Jersey," says Mattie Houlden. "There was a terrible storm raging that night, almost hurricane-force gales and pounding rain." Worse, her pickup was light and tended to sway in the wind.

As she traveled, gusts kept pushing the truck off the road. Mattie prayed for help every time she wrestled the vehicle back onto the pavement. Her shoulders ached by the time she approached a shortcut. Should she take it? It would get her home sooner, but the route was deserted.

Another blast rocked the truck, and Mattie made a decision. Turning, she skidded onto the rough road, straightened out the wheel—then looked in amazement at the scene. There was no rain beating on her windshield, no howling wind, nothing except a quiet starry night. Mattie drove home completely content.

"I know storms don't end at corners," she says, "so I had only God to thank."

Vic* had been donating five percent of his take-home pay to the poor. But when his family hit a rough financial period, Vic was tempted to stop; wasn't his first obligation to them? "God," he finally said, "I'll keep taking care of your poor, but please let me know that you'll keep taking care of us!"

The following weekend, Vic pulled into a gas station to fill up. Only then did he realize he had forgotten to do so last Saturday. Although his car uses exactly one tank of gas each week, it had somehow run for seven extra days on Empty.

It was the reassurance Vic needed. He could never outdo God in generosity.

Ray* told Radio Station WEZE listeners in Boston what happened to him the morning after a snowstorm. "I tried several times to make a phone call, but the line was dead," he said. "So I looked at the snow on the front walk and decided to go out and shovel."

As Ray pulled on his boots, the telephone rang. It was his brother, and they talked briefly. Ray was glad that the telephone service had been restored. He hung up and opened the door.

"There, lying across my path, was a live electrical wire," he said. "It had obviously fallen during the moment I was on the phone. I would have been right under it if my brother hadn't called."

Ray picked up the phone to call his brother to tell him about his near miss. But the phone was dead again. And it remained out of service for the rest of the weekend.

"Monday morning, when the telephone crew came, I told the foreman that I had received one call on Saturday," Ray said.

The foreman gave him an odd look. "You couldn't have," he said. "No one in this area has had telephone service since Friday night. The lines were completely destroyed during the storm."

Then Ray knew Who had temporarily repaired the wires, just for him.

We marvel at God's authority in thunder and wind, His gentleness in a delicate leaf, a tiny ant. He made the universe, and He commands every portion of it.

And under ordinary circumstances, His laws of science and logic prevail. Gravity, weather conditions, cars, telephone wires, and other mechanical items operate in a certain order. Matter doesn't reproduce. People aren't in two places at once. But when miracles happen, God can and does suspend such laws.

Why would God do it? Perhaps to show both His power and His love. A group of scientists recently examined the *tilma* or cape of Juan Diego, a poor Inca Indian who claimed to have seen the Virgin Mary in 1534. On the *tilma* is an image of Mary, later called Our Lady of Guadeloupe. The *tilma* is made out of cactus cloth, a material that should have disintegrated a few centuries ago. Yet it is still whole and beautiful. One of the scientists' comments sums up the following stories:

"God made nature, and God can manipulate nature any way He chooses."

Tender Treasures

> Miracles do not happen in contradiction to nature,
> but only in contradiction to what is known to us of
> nature.
>
> SAINT AUGUSTINE

A reader, feeling abandoned and lonely, looked out of her hotel window at a magnolia tree, its buds tightly closed. How she wished God would send a signal to her that He was near and heard the longings of her heart! Suddenly, as she watched in disbelief, one bud moved, then opened quickly and completely in a glorious array of color and beauty. *I still have a photograph of that lone flower on the tree,* she wrote. *God works many small miracles, but most have to be seen with the heart.*

Nancy Trant, mourning the sudden death of her fiancé, traveled to Colorado where they had planned to honeymoon. The trip was picturesque but very lonely.

One day Nancy rented a car and drove to the top of Pikes Peak, some fourteen thousand feet above sea level. At the summit, however, she began to feel dizzy. The entire peak was covered in a dense cloud. "Since no one else was around and I couldn't see anything, I started back to my car," she says.

On the way, she heard an inner voice command: "Return to where you were standing." Still light-headed, Nancy argued with the voice, but it remained insistent within her spirit: "Go!" Relenting, she hiked back to the guardrail.

Instantly, the clouds parted in front of her. "Before me stood a rainbow three to four stories high, coming out of the mountain and reaching into infinity," Nancy says. The air seemed tinged with electricity, and she could see for miles. Nancy was transfixed, filled with rapture. Wasn't the rainbow a sign of God's covenant with His people, with her? The exquisite scene remained for several minutes, then clouds covered the summit again. But Nancy has never forgotten the moment when God sent her consolation in her grief and the promise of a happier tomorrow.

As she ran errands with her children, Kaylyn Dunne was lost in thought. She had just returned from a weekend retreat that used the butterfly, a universal symbol of change and metamorphosis, as its theme. The retreat had aroused her desire for a deeper spiritual life, yet worried her too, because she had been asked to be the chairperson of subsequent retreats. Kaylyn had never been chairperson of anything, and she felt quite inadequate. With her already-crowded schedule and a chronically ill son to care for, would God want her to do this?

"Mom, look!" her son suddenly exclaimed from the backseat. Kaylyn almost hit the brakes. Walking in front of her, inside the car, was a huge monarch butterfly. It was a vivid yellow, her favorite color. With the car moving at forty-five miles per hour and the windows open barely a crack—her preteen daughters didn't want their hair blown about—how had it gotten in?

The winged visitor fluttered around delicately, then landed, like a little puff, on the dashboard. Awed, the children stared at it. "It must be frightened," Kaylyn told them. "Open the windows and let it fly out." Yet, despite the wind, the butterfly stayed.

Kaylyn pulled into the library parking lot. "Let's leave the windows down while we're gone," she suggested. When they returned to the car, however, the monarch was still sitting gracefully on the dashboard, as if awaiting them.

Bemused, Kaylyn finished the errands, drove home, opened the car doors, went into the house with the children and waited. Eventually the butterfly leisurely emerged, circled the house in a kind of embrace, and flew off.

"I got to thinking about the timeliness of its arrival, right after I had prayed," Kaylyn says. Did God intend it as a signal that He was near? Kaylyn accepted the chairperson job, and it became her path to a richer spiritual life.

Since that day, butterflies seem to visit Kaylyn often, especially when she needs encouragement. One of the best encounters came last winter. As friends held a prayer service for Kaylyn's son in her living room, someone pointed toward the front window and exclaimed, "Look outside!"

The January day was snowy and subzero. But tapping gently against the glass—as if reminding Kaylyn of God's constant care—was a brown butterfly.

Flowers, rainbows, butterflies . . . nature's most tender treasures. Perhaps God uses them to bridge the barriers between heaven and earth, to let us know that as He watches the sparrow, He surely watches us.

The Lord of
Wind and Flame

*The men were amazed and asked, "What kind of man
is this? Even the winds and the seas obey him!"*

MATTHEW 8:27

$\mathcal{I}$t was June 1984, and Alberta McCreery and her friend
Louise were visiting Louise's relatives in Lewis, Kansas. Suddenly Louise's sister-in-law dashed into the living room, pale
and frightened. "The wheat fields are on fire!" she cried.

The fields lay just between them and the town's school. As
the women ran outside, they could hear crackling and see
smoke billowing in the air. "Kansas winds are strong and
constant, especially across open plains," Alberta explains. And
with the wheat still uncut, fire would soon turn the fields into
a tinderbox of destruction.

Everyone's first thought was to get to Grandma, who was
almost immobile with arthritis—and home alone. "Pray,
Alberta!" Louise shouted over her shoulder, running down
the road to Grandma's house. Now they could see the flames,
whipped by high winds, sweeping toward the school buildings.

What an inferno! It would be minutes before fire trucks could arrive, and by then the buildings would be engulfed. People were running and yelling, but Alberta looked upward, asking God to send protection. "With my hands aloft, racing down the street, I called upon the angels to calm the winds and bring the fire under control," she says.

At this point, Grandma had come out of her house and down the stairs, Louise had grabbed a garden hose, and sirens were sounding in the distance. "Then an astonishing thing happened," Alberta says. "The wind—that unceasing, ever-blowing Kansas wind—died down. Suddenly and completely." The entire atmosphere seemed hushed. Even the birds stopped singing. Not a whisper of breeze touched Alberta's cheeks.

In just a few seconds, with no draft to fan it, the fire stopped its onward rush. Instead of moving across the fields, it burned straighter and slower. By the time the trucks arrived, it was under control, just yards from the school buildings.

"We gave fervent thanks to the unseen forces who swept into action at our call," Alberta says. "They do move in a mysterious way!"

For many years, Carol Rosen lived in a house along the ridge of a hill in San Diego. Whenever she left it, she would bless it, thank God for protecting it, and picture it surrounded in white light.

During one especially dry September, Carol attended a spiritual retreat in Idyllwild, a town near Palm Springs. "During my stay, I was suddenly shown a vision of my house with a large cross of white light over the top of it," she says. "I had no idea what this meant, but I knew it was good, so I thanked God and blessed my home again."

A few days later she drove back to San Diego, feeling rested and refreshed despite the over ninety degrees temperature and a hot and heavy Santa Ana wind. Almost home, however, she looked up—and saw her entire hill enveloped in flames, black smoke billowing upward. "I didn't dare go up any farther," Carol says. "I parked at the foot of the drive, and stood there and prayed." The hill would be a total loss, she knew, especially in that drought.

Fire trucks didn't arrive until several minutes later. The firefighters ran up the hill in their asbestos gear, lugging heavy hoses, but it was obviously too late. There was too much smoke and flames for Carol to see the destruction. But the fierce Santa Ana winds would have spread the fires quickly.

Yet when the first firefighters came down from the hill, they were incredulous. "We put out the fire," one told Carol. "Not one home was touched—on either hill. Everything is safe. We can't understand it."

"Then I understood what the cross of light I had seen meant," Carol says. "We were all being divinely protected."

Angel
in the Tree

*All I have seen teaches me to trust the Creator for all
I have not seen.*

RALPH WALDO EMERSON

*D*uring World War II, young Mildred Lee moved in with her
parents when her soldier-husband was sent overseas. Mildred's
five-year-old daughter, Genevieve, enjoyed being the apple of
her grandparents' eyes. But Mildred worried about her husband, so far away. Would he be killed? How could she manage
without him?

One evening the stress evidently became too great. Little
Genevieve awakened to the sound of her mother screaming
and trying to climb out of her bedroom window. "There's an
angel in the tree," Mildred kept crying. "An angel outside our
house!"

It took both her distraught parents to restrain her from
leaping out the window. "She's huge, in a shiny dress, with
the most beautiful light around her," Mildred wept. "She'll
protect us—I know she will. Please let me go to her!"

There *were* two ancient horse-chestnut trees in front of the house, one on each side of the road. But certainly no one had ever seen an angel in either. And in the 1940s, people who had "visions" needed protective care. Mildred was taken to a mental hospital and, over the next two years, received thirty-six shock treatments to cure what everyone assumed was a nervous breakdown.

Genevieve's father came home safely from the war, collected his daughter, and moved to a nearby town. Then Mildred was released from the hospital. "She came to us a different person, very childlike," says Genevieve, "and Dad and I began a life of caring for her."

In those days, no one acknowledged mental illness. Everyone in the family simply pretended nothing was different about Mildred. But at least once a day, when no one was around to overhear, Mildred would tell young Genevieve how special they were, because a beautiful angel was watching over them. "I can't see her now, because she's in your grandparents' tree," Mildred would say, "but I know she's there."

At seventeen, Genevieve left home to marry Jim Weaver. At about the same time, her parents moved in to care for her ailing grandparents, back to the house where Mildred had seen the angel. Apparently the angel was still there.

"As the years passed, my mother talked to and about the angel more often," Genevieve recalls. If someone dropped by, Mildred happily described the angel's clothes or the beautiful light around her. Relatives and neighbors sat on the porch in the shadow of the huge tree, wearing earnest expressions as they listened to the stories and watched the rapturous look on Mildred's face. Gradually they formed a tender conspiracy. What did it matter if their innocent, vulnerable Mildred had hallucinations? Who was she harming? And it was a nice thought, wasn't it—an angel watching over the house?

Genevieve's grandparents died, and then her father. Suddenly she had full responsibility for her mother's care. It was easier to move Mildred into Genevieve's busy household than the other way around, and that is what she did. But Mildred was like a lost soul, grieving for the angel left behind.

"There were nights when I would drive the twenty miles back to my grandparents' house, which was still unsold, and sit inside and cry over the situation," Genevieve says. "I missed my father, and I didn't know what to do about my mother's unhappiness. Yet sometimes I sensed that the answers were in the house itself, and that everything was going to be all right." Eventually she and Jim decided to sell their house and move Mildred back with them to the place she had always loved.

Mildred was ecstatic. Once again, she sat on the familiar porch, singing hymns and talking to the angel in the shadow of her beloved chestnut tree. "Soon I will go to be with her and with your father," she would tell Genevieve. Genevieve felt serene too. The house, even the tree, seemed to welcome her, comfort her. Their decision had been a good one.

On September 9, 1989, Mildred died. Just a few weeks later, Jim came through the front door wearing a puzzled expression. "Have you looked at that tree?" he asked his wife.

"Mom's tree?" Genevieve hadn't. But when she went to the window, she was dumbfounded.

At the funeral, both huge chestnuts had been heavily leafed. Now, although the one across the street was still robust, the Weavers' tree was a black skeleton, withered and lifeless.

"What happened?" Jim was asking. "Healthy trees don't die overnight."

Genevieve looked at it. Like a faithful guardian, it had spread its shadow across her entire family. And within its boughs, her mother had found peace. Genevieve would miss the tree, she knew. But its job was done.

Miracles in
Multiples

*By miracles we don't mean contradictions to nature.
We mean that, left to her own resources, she could
never produce them.*

C. S. LEWIS, *MIRACLES*

T he Jewish feast Chanukah, the Festival of Lights, celebrates a Biblical event when a one-day supply of oil burned for eight days to protect God's people. Jesus multiplied loaves and fishes to feed his followers, on more than one occasion. And apparently God continues to make something out of nothing when His people require it.

In El Paso, Texas, such a phenomenon started in 1972 when members of a small prayer group read a Bible passage about preparing for a banquet. "When you give a banquet, invite the poor, the crippled, the lame, the blind, and you will be blessed," it said (Luke 14:13). The group, led by Father Richard Thomas, decided to share Christmas dinner with Mexican trash grubbers and their families in Juárez, Mexico, destitute people who support themselves by selling items dug from the garbage pits across the Rio Grande.

It took the prayer group several days to prepare a bountiful table. But word had spread, and the guests from Juárez numbered more than three hundred, twice as many as expected. Yet there was plenty of food. Puzzled, the volunteer assigned to slice the hams reported that they stayed the same size, although each guest received a generous portion. Tamales seemed to multiply in their serving bowls. When everyone had eaten, leftovers in abundance were given to the guests to take home.

Members of the prayer group were baffled. But, encouraged by the bounty inexplicably provided for them on Christmas, they decided to continue what they had begun, reaching out with both material and spiritual help to their Juárez neighbors. Gradually, things began to change. Long-standing feuds among the trash grubbers diminished, replaced by reconciliation and healing. Volunteers from both cities built a food and fish ranch, a brickyard, a water cistern. Physical healings became common. Spiritual conversions abounded. And the multiplication of food and supplies?

It continues to this day. Tortilla flour, grapes from the farm, cans of condensed milk for children—even lime for plastering buildings—all these commodities and more have mysteriously increased, witnesses attest. "The multiplications are not that frequent and certainly not predictable," Father Thomas explains. "And although we try to keep records, it is a feeble attempt. Frankly, we just don't have the help to keep track of all the miracles God does here."[12]

Eileen Freeman, author of *Touched by Angels,* had a similar experience while a college student at Barnard. During the summer of 1969 she lived with a small prayer community in Ann Arbor, Michigan. The men and women roomed in separate houses but came together for dinner. "We all contributed to the grocery bill, and each night one person cooked," Eileen says. "Guests were always welcome too, whether they were part of the academic community or passers-by in need of a meal."

One evening, Eileen went to fix dinner and found only a two-pound package of ground beef in the freezer. Although she added plenty of bread crumbs and other "stretch" ingredients, the meat loaf would be barely enough to give each of the twelve a small slice. And what if unexpected company arrived?

Just as everyone was about to sit down, a station wagon pulled into the driveway, and several young men jumped out. They had just completed a long retreat at Boston College and, eager to share their joyful experiences with the Ann Arbor community, had driven nearly eight hundred miles without stopping.

Of course they were invited to dinner. Eileen took a quick head count. Nineteen! She got out more bread, made another pitcher of Kool-Aid, and joined the others for a fervent blessing on the food. Someone sliced the meat loaf and passed the platter around.

"It was a wonderful dinner, with the guests sharing stories of how they had come to know Jesus better during their retreat," Eileen recalls. There was prayer and singing and laughter. And amazingly, there was meat loaf. The platter was half full when everyone reached for second helpings, still half full when some took a third. Surprised and overjoyed, the young people gave thanks for God's presence in their midst.

And it hadn't ended yet. There was even enough meat loaf for sandwiches the following day.

What if it's not the *quantity* but the *quality* that needs changing? Pat Mullins is the leader of Ephesians 1:4, a prayer group with five hundred members in Dublin, California. People often help one another with projects, so when Pat had to paint the inside of a house his daughter would be renting, an airline pilot, a retired teacher, a building contractor, and several other "nice, normal people" from the prayer group volunteered to help.

"I was short on cash, and since the contractor always has cans of leftover paint stored in his shed, he told us to take what we needed," Pat says. "I wanted the same neutral color throughout the house so, using a can of white base, I added a few ounces of blue, the rest of a pint of peach. . . . Eventually I got a nice shade that I thought would do the job."

It didn't. Only halfway through the rooms, the paint ran out. The workers looked at one another. What now? There was no possibility the same color could be duplicated, not with the first batch's slapdash mixing. And the only base color remaining was apricot, hardly a neutral shade.

Nevertheless, everyone went back into the shed and began mixing, stirring—and praying, hoping they would not have to repaint everything in a new tint. "People in a prayer community get used to working things out with God," Pat says. "We always assume that whatever He's doing is perfect, and although it might be nice if He'd do it *this* way, we're willing to obey."

The workers' prayers were answered. For, despite using different proportions and colors, the new paint turned out to be the *exact* shade as the previous batch. "A professional would not be able to tell where we stopped and started again," Pat says.

It's natural to want to provide for our own needs. But sometimes we have to lean on God. And "when we are willing to let Him be our source and resource," Pat points out, "the results are always delightful."

*   *   *

Does multiplication happen only in groups? Patricia Story says no. A native New Yorker, she lived in an affluent suburb on Long Island until 1977, when her husband was transferred to Albuquerque. The family looked forward to the change. They bought land on a picturesque seven-thousand-foot elevation near the San Pedro Mountains and put a double-wide mobile home on it until they could build a house.

But their dreams began to sour. Pat's husband developed diabetes, and his company fired him. He started a business with their house fund, and in 1985 he died suddenly from an aneurysm. Only after the funeral did Pat discover he had borrowed on his remaining life-insurance policy and had also run up substantial debts.

Pat kept the business afloat for a few years, and she managed to pay off most of the debts. But she couldn't move to an apart-ment—and an easier lifestyle—because rents were too high. Her now-grown children had trouble finding jobs, especially during the winter when freezing weather complicated every-thing. Gradually, Pat developed health problems. "I, who once had a nine-room house, vacations, jewelry, now worried about paying the electric bill or the doctor," she says. Pat had always been a lukewarm Christian, but now she began to pray.

In February 1992, Pat got a $197 water bill and discovered a leak under the trailer in her hot-water heater. "With four feet of snow, I certainly hadn't noticed it," she says. But she couldn't pay the bill, so the water was turned off. Once a day, the family filled jugs with snow to heat for washing and cooking.

On March 30, Pat took her regular delivery of one hundred gallons of propane gas for heating in an outside pressurized tank. If she used it very sparingly, it might last two months. And then what would she do? There was no money for more.

She looked around her trailer. Broken appliances, cars junked, she herself exhausted in body and spirit. . . . Perhaps that was the moment when Pat threw herself completely on God. "I can't do any more," she told Him. "You said You would provide, and You have to do it."

A few weeks later, Pat's son brought her an armload of roses. "I got some yard work in town, trimming bushes," he told her. "These would have been thrown away."

Pat loved flowers, and she hadn't had any for years. She put them where she could enjoy their glorious fragrance. They seemed more than just flowers, somehow—almost a sign that something good was about to happen.

A week later, the flowers died, and while disposing of them, Pat remembered to check the propane tank. When she looked at the gauge, she was incredulous. There were still ninety gallons remaining, even though it should be registering less than half full. Was the gauge broken? The gas company said no, adding that Pat just wasn't using much fuel.

But she hadn't altered her routine. Yet months passed, and the gauge stayed almost in the same spot. With large fuel costs absent, Pat started catching up—and other little oddities occurred. When her expensive eyeglasses broke, her daughter bought her a pair for $11.95 that worked better than any Pat had previously owned. Another daughter found a job just as everyone needed new clothes. After a fall, Pat learned that she had broken a bone in her leg—but it had somehow healed by itself. And the propane kept coming.

Finally, in November, nine months after her last order, Pat took another shipment of fuel for winter. "I gave you less than usual because you still have some left from last year," the deliveryman commented. "Funny, isn't it?"

Not funny, Pat feels. Miraculous. And the real marvel may not be the propane as much as her own growing trust, born out of surrender to God. "I don't know what the future holds for us, but we are all closer to God," she says. "I have developed a strong prayer life. And when I can share something, I do. I'm learning that it always comes back one hundredfold."

There had never been a time when Bonnie Rose Loveall hadn't felt alone. Family members had either died or abandoned her when she was very young, and because she was now a single mother of two small children, others disapproved of her. Bonnie received a bit of state aid in the form of food coupons, but she never had any cash. In fact, for years, she says, "I carried a one-dollar bill in my wallet to remind myself I was a human being."

It was during this bleak and difficult period that Bonnie became aware of a Higher Power. She had never known God, but one day, she says, "I asked for help to raise my children." Was this how one prayed? She had nobody to talk it over with, and her solitary life continued.

It was always a struggle to keep food on the table, especially when she ran out of coupons. But one Sunday night, Bonnie looked at her almost-bare cabinets with real concern. How was she going to feed the kids until the end of this week? There were no kindly neighbors to lend her anything, no local food bank—just herself and the rapidly emptying refrigerator.

Usually something turned up, but this week, nothing did. By lunchtime on Tuesday, Bonnie was completely out of food. Forcing herself to remain calm, she checked every cupboard, every drawer in her tiny apartment, even looking under the beds. But there was nothing to eat. The children were crying from hunger, and Bonnie pondered the situation. She had no one to turn to, no one at all, but God. Yet her faith was so weak. . . . She took a deep breath. "God, the children need food," she said simply.

Immediately Bonnie felt an inner urge to look in the cupboards again. She resisted. Hadn't she already searched the bare shelves, to no avail? But again, something stirred her, and this time she opened a cabinet.

"There was a box of macaroni and cheese sitting there," Bonnie recalls. "I knew it had not been there earlier, and I felt shocked and grateful." Quickly she cooked the contents, and she and the children ate and ate.

The pan still seemed full of macaroni. Bonnie put it into the refrigerator, ready to warm up again for supper. God had provided her daily bread after all.

The macaroni fed them again that evening. But there was still almost a full pan remaining. Bonnie refrigerated it again that night, and the next night . . . and the next. . . . "We ate out of that pan for an entire week, until I was able to buy food again," she says. "I knew I was having a supernatural experience. But who could I tell?"

Bonnie never wondered why God didn't furnish a banquet rather than a humble box of macaroni. "I think my faith then— and now—is like a child's, in that I just take what is provided at face value," she says. "I had told God my problems, and I left the outcome to Him."

Always Near

Coincidence is God's way of remaining anonymous.

TRADITIONAL SAYING

*E*ileen Bosshart of Streamwood, Illinois, was in the middle of a dilemma. She had run out of a major ingredient for tonight's dinner, and if she ran to the store for it, the meal would be late—and she'd be even later for tonight's choir practice. Oh, there were times when it was difficult being the mother of nine! Eileen's days were spent chauffeuring children in all directions, while trying to keep up with housework and her own projects—editing a newsletter, teaching religion classes, helping to run a food pantry in an inner-city parish, and, at this particular time, planning a dinner dance to raise funds for a missionary priest. "I tried to fit in as many activities as I could in a day," Eileen says (in modest understatement). "But I always seemed to be rushing."

Now she searched through kitchen cabinets, slamming doors and pulling out drawers. Surely she could find something to substitute! The thought of another errand at this busy time of day was too much to contemplate.

But her hopeful search yielded nothing, so the supermarket

dash was inevitable. The youngest, four-year-old Allison, had been watching Eileen's frenetic search and now realized that Mom was going out. "Can I come with you, Mommy?" Eagerly the little girl ran to the back door.

Eileen couldn't let herself be slowed down by a preschooler. Time was crucial. If she could get to the store, find what she needed in a hurry, and race home, she could resume her fast track without too much of a loss. "Not now, Allison." Eileen brushed past her daughter. "You stay here and watch television with Danny and Mark. I'll take you another time, when I'm not in such a hurry."

The station wagon was parked in the driveway. Her thoughts scattered, Eileen rushed out, climbed in, and started the engine. Quickly she shifted into reverse. At least, she *tried* to, but the gear seemed to be stuck. She tried again, pulling with all her might, but the lever wouldn't move. Oh no, not *now,* not when she most needed to save time! Why did everything seem to go wrong when she was in a hurry?

At that moment, Eileen heard a little tapping sound. And as she looked through the rearview mirror, time seemed to stand still. The top of Allison's blond head was barely visible through the back window, but Eileen could see her daughter standing directly behind the station wagon, almost against it. Had the gear not stuck, she would have roared backward down the driveway, right over her child.

"Oh, Allison!" Eileen stumbled out of the car, scooped up her daughter and put her in the front seat. What a near miss! "I sat and held her and prayed for a couple of minutes, until I felt my strength coming back," Eileen says. "Then I put the car in reverse again. The gear moved easily, and we backed safely out of the driveway."

Was it just a coincidence that the reverse gear stuck once— and never again, despite mechanical checks, during many additional years of driving? "I know that God is attentive to us whether we are consciously thinking of Him or not," Eileen says. "I'll be forever grateful that He spared us all from such a tragedy."

In the Midst
of Battle

Ah, fondest, blindest, weakest,
I am He Whom thou seekest!

FRANCIS THOMPSON,
"THE HOUND OF HEAVEN"

*B*y the time Albert Leo entered college and began studying for a career in science, he was ready to discredit organized religions. But God was still at work in his life. "As time passed, I kept having experiences that could not be explained by science," Albert says. "It became clear to me that *all* of reality cannot be placed under a microscope, sent through a cyclotron, or bombarded with electromagnetic radiation to be measured, plotted, and classified."

Albert, however, was still a self-described "hardheaded G.I." in 1944 when he and his fellow infantrymen slogged through the snow and mud of the Vosges Mountains. They had fought some smaller skirmishes with the German army, but casualties had been high. Nearly one-fourth of their company was now sick, wounded, or dead. "Usually, we'd march through the night, attack a German-held town at dawn, then occupy houses and dig defensive positions on the outskirts," Albert explains.

Toward the end of December, the company commander decided to change methods. A night patrol would penetrate the next town, Linxgen, and capture prisoners for interrogation. Albert was one of the two advance scouts.

Albert had already had a number of close calls. But that evening he experienced a deep foreboding, a certainty that he wouldn't be coming back. So strong was the feeling that he left his valuables behind with a buddy.

Instead of helmets, the two soldiers put on white parkas so that they would blend in with the snow. Then, carrying grenade launchers, they inched down the half-mile hill from the line to a house. It was empty, so they signaled the rest of the squad to move up and around it. "Remember, *one* blow on my whistle means you return to the house," the squad leader reminded everyone. "*Two* blasts means everyone retreats to the line."

Albert and the other scout pressed forward again, moving in a half crouch now across two hundred yards of open area toward the village.

"Albert!" the other scout whispered about two-thirds of the way across. "I saw something. I'm going back to talk to the squad leader."

"Sure." While the other scout made his way back to the house, Albert lay motionless, hoping he couldn't be seen. Soon rifle fire sounded in front of him from the village wall. The first few rounds didn't come close to Albert.

He was sure he was sufficiently camouflaged, but since there was a woodpile to his left, he decided to run for it. Just as he did, something flashed from the wall, and a second later, his whole world burst into blazing stars. Albert felt himself being lifted from the waist. *So this is how it feels to get hit!* he thought. Strangely, as he slipped into darkness, he felt no panic, no deep regrets, just peace and . . . the presence of God.

Time passed. Dimly Albert realized that he wasn't dead after all, but still lying in the snow. Gradually, he moved different parts of his body and discovered that his right arm didn't work. With his left, Albert pushed back his parka hood and clumsily shoved some snow onto his throbbing right temple. He had probably sustained a minor flesh wound. If he had been wearing a helmet rather than the parka, he probably wouldn't have been injured at all. Bad luck.

Firing had stopped, and Albert seemed to be the only human on the silent landscape. Somehow he managed to crawl the remaining distance to the woodpile and prop himself up behind it. Any minute one of his buddies would rescue him. It was just a matter of staying conscious until then.

But he heard nothing, not until a piercing whistle broke the silence. One blast.

Albert's heart sank. His company commander was calling the scouts back to the house. When Albert didn't show up, everyone would assume the rifle fire had killed him. A few moments later, Albert's worst fears were realized. The whistle blew twice. His squad was moving back to the line, leaving him alone.

Well, almost alone. Somewhere behind the wall there was still the German soldier who had shot him. Twenty minutes passed without a sound. Albert's head wound was still bleeding, and he knew he could freeze to death. Surrender was probably his only option. In his best high school German, he called into the stillness: "I need help! I'm ready to give up!"

No one answered.

Did the enemy soldier think it was a trap? Albert couldn't blame him. But he couldn't wait until morning to surrender, either. By then, the German would find only a corpse. Instead, Albert stood up behind the woodpile and, to his great surprise, found he could walk. Then, why surrender? Maybe he could make it back to his company.

Weaving, staggering, sometimes falling, Albert made it to the empty house. Panting, he collapsed on the ground for a moment and pushed more snow onto the wound in his forehead. Then, dragging himself upright, he wobbled down the hill. "I wasn't sure of the route back and had forgotten the password," he says. "So I kept calling out that I was a G.I. and needed help."

No one responded.

The exhausting journey seemed to take forever. Through his pain and fear, Albert heard gunfire from where he had come. But finally an arm reached out of the darkness. "Come on, buddy," a voice said. "I'll help you to the aid station." He had made it!

Later, the hospital doctor asked Albert what had happened. And when Albert described his journey, the doctor smiled and shook his head. "No way, soldier. Someone must have carried you. There's not one chance in a hundred thousand that you could have walked alone back to the line."

"Why not?" Albert asked. "It was just a flesh wound, wasn't it?"

"A flesh wound! The hole in your skull was three inches across. If you had been wearing a helmet instead of a parka, that piece of shrapnel would have bounced under the metal and killed you."

Albert was confounded. And he had thought the parka was bad luck!

"Anyway, soldier, you couldn't have remained conscious, not with your head open," the doctor continued. "And if you had passed out for any length of time, you would have died from shock, loss of blood, or freezing. Nope." He shook his head. "There's no explanation for why you're going to live."

Albert lay back, eyes wide. He was thinking of what the other scout had told him, moments after he had collapsed behind the line, when Albert had gasped, "Why didn't you give me some covering fire?"

"We would have, but we didn't know how many Germans were behind the pillbox," the other scout had explained. "We all went back to the line to fire on it."

"There wasn't any pillbox around," Albert had argued.

"Yes, there was—just to the left of you."

"That was a *woodpile!*" Albert exclaimed. "The shots came from the wall, not there—I hid behind it, waiting for you."

The two soldiers looked at each other. "We fired on it," the other scout said softly. "If you had still been there, we would have killed you."

Today Albert Leo is a project director at the Seaver Chemistry Laboratory in Claremont, California, still deeply scientific, and deeply spiritual as well. And from time to time he remembers the episode in Linxgen. Was it just a coincidence that he was wearing a parka rather than a helmet, that the snow he packed into a seemingly fatal head wound kept him alive? Was it only *his* legs that carried him over two hundred open yards, then a half-mile up a snow-covered hill? "Where and how do we encounter God?" Albert asks. "He is present when we least expect Him."

On Butterfly Wings

"You're writing a book about miracles?" Nancy Montonaro had a typically hesitant look on her face. "My aunt and uncle had an experience— Well, you'll probably laugh, but the family has always wondered. . . ."

"Tell me," I prompted. And Nancy did.

Her Aunt Evelyn and Uncle Harvey had shared a long and happy marriage. Then Harvey went into the hospital, complaining of pain. The couple was stunned when Harvey's doctor diagnosed terminal bone cancer. How would they cope, not only with Harvey's physical deterioration, but with the sorrow that such a loss was already creating?

Harvey came home, but it was a difficult time. He grew thin, less able to move around. Privately Evelyn prayed that the end would come swiftly, that her beloved and valiant husband wouldn't have to endure his anguish much longer. Wrapped in grief, each longed for consolation, but neither could give it to the other.

One pleasant summer morning Harvey decided to sit for a while in the backyard. Immediately after he settled in his chair, he noticed a huge blue butterfly hovering just above him. No, there were *two* blue butterflies bobbing gracefully around his chair. Harvey hardly moved a muscle, hoping they would stay within view for a moment. The species must be rare—he had never seen anything like them.

The winged creatures didn't fly away. Instead, both came closer, closer. Harvey held his breath. What were they doing? Incredibly, one landed gently on his bare hand. The other came and perched on his shoulder.

Instantly, Harvey was flooded with a feeling of serenity and pleasure. The sun was warm, the day glorious—and the butter-flies settled down as if they were enjoying it right along with him. Tentatively Harvey studied the one on his hand. Why, he could see each tiny vein in the sapphire-blue wing, even make out the butterfly's miniature eyes and mouth. It was incredible.

Captivated, Evelyn watched the strange scene. Where had these brilliant beings come from? She often worked in the garden, but she had never seen anything like them. Intrigued and wanting a closer look, she quietly opened the kitchen door and stepped outside. Immediately, although they could hardly have seen or heard her, the butterflies darted away, out of their view. "Oh, I've frightened them!" she said, disappointed.

"You did see them, didn't you?" Harvey asked. "I had thought I was imagining things. Weren't they splendid?"

Evelyn looked at her husband. He seemed almost serene. Obviously, the butterflies had worked a kind of healing on his spirit. If only they would return! But chances of that were slim.

The next day Harvey went into the yard again. And, as if they had been waiting for him, the two blue butterflies appeared, fluttered, and daintily took their places—one on Harvey's hand, the other on his shoulder. Harvey was amazed and enchanted. But the moment Evelyn attempted to come into the yard, the creatures flew away.

The scenario continued as the days passed. If Evelyn or anyone else was in the yard, the winged visitors remained hidden from view. If they were with Harvey and a neighbor approached, they would quickly float away. But whenever Harvey sat alone in his chair, he had only to wait a moment, and they appeared. And not just for an instant. Incredibly, the butterflies stayed as long as Harvey did. "It's as if they're guarding me," he once told his wife. "I feel so protected, so loved."

Harvey was growing frailer as his illness progressed, and Evelyn knew his pain was increasing too. But she had prayed for consolation and peace for both of them, and their spirits were indeed lighter. The butterflies had been the perfect answer.

Harvey entered the hospital that fall and died soon afterward. And although Evelyn occasionally sat in Harvey's chair, hoping to woo the butterflies back to the yard, no one ever saw them again. It was as if their assignment was over. They had stood faithfully on guard, and then they had escorted their charge safely home.

Miracle at the Mall

When I pray, coincidences happen,
When I stop praying, coincidences stop.

WILLIAM TEMPLE, ARCHBISHOP OF CANTERBURY

Occasionally, a story's origins can't be completely traced. But people who knew the late Howard Conatser, founder of the Beverly Hills Baptist Church in Dallas, recall his integrity. They know he would have to be personally convinced that an event was authentic before sharing it with others. His widow, Helen, and some members of his former congregation now attend Church on the Rock South in Duncanville, Texas, and remember this story well.

"Howard heard it—possibly from the father himself—at a Christian convention in California in the late '70s," Helen Conatser says. The pastor came home and told the story to others, including a nationwide television audience during a sermon. "A lot of miraculous things seemed to be happening in our congregation and to people we knew at that time," says Helen. "This was just one more, so we accepted it as a gift from God, and never felt the need to try and prove it." Hence, the trail has come to an end. But the wonder remains.

*   *   *

Beth* and Margie*, two teenage sisters, had enjoyed shopping in the large enclosed mall. But by the time they were ready to leave, it was dark. Standing at the mall exit, they could hardly see the outline of their car, the only one left in that section of the dimly lit parking lot.

The girls were nervous as they waited, hoping a few customers would come along so they could all walk out together. Both were aware of the current crime wave. There had been muggings and rapes in area shopping malls, and they remembered their father's warning: "Don't stay too late!"

"Dad's going to be furious," Beth said.

"Then we'd better get going—now!" Margie shifted her packages, pushed open the door, and walked as fast as she could. Beth followed, glancing from side to side. Street traffic had subsided, but the lot seemed a bit *too* quiet.

They had made it! Beth shoved the key into the car lock, got in, and reached across to open Margie's door. Just then the girls heard the sound of running feet behind them. When Margie turned around, her heart almost stopped. Racing toward them were two ominous-looking men.

"You're not going anywhere!" one shouted.

Margie screamed. Terrified, she scrambled inside, and both girls locked their doors, just in time.

With shaking fingers, Beth turned on the car's ignition switch. Nothing happened. She did it again, and again. But only the sound of the key clicked in the silence. They had no power!

"Beth, try again!" Margie was frantic. The men were pulling the door handles, pushing at the windows.

"I can't!" Beth cried. "It won't start!"

The girls knew there were only seconds of safety remaining. Quickly, they joined hands in prayer.

"Dear God," Margie pleaded, "give us a miracle, in the name of Jesus!"

Once more, Beth turned the key. This time the engine roared to life. She shifted into gear and raced out of the parking lot, leaving the men behind.

The girls wept all the way home, shocked and relieved at the same time. They screeched down the driveway to the garage, stumbled into the safety of their house, and told their father what had happened. He held them both close.

"You're safe—that's the main thing," he soothed them. "But you could have been hurt or even killed. Don't ever put yourself in that kind of situation again!"

"We won't," Margie promised, wiping her eyes.

Her father was frowning. "It's strange, though. The car has never failed to start. I'll check it out tomorrow."

Early the next morning, he raised the car's hood to look at the starter. And in one stunned glance, he realized Who had brought his daughters safely home the previous night.

For there was no battery in the car.

The Last Christmas Gift

Come ye blessed children of my Father, receive the kingdom prepared for you from the beginning of the world.

THE BOOK OF COMMON PRAYER

$\mathcal{S}$now had been predicted. But twelve-year-old Betty Wohlfert (now Roberts) and her ten-year-old sister, Leonie, didn't give it a thought on that late afternoon in 1924, when they sneaked out with the sled they had just received for Christmas. "Dad thought we were in the house helping Mama, and she thought we were in the barn doing chores for Dad," Betty says. Instead the girls went to a hill near their farm in Hubbardston, Michigan.

Exhilarated and breathless, neither noticed snowflakes starting to fall—until the moon disappeared and gale-force winds began to blow across the darkening plains. Abruptly, they found themselves in the midst of a blinding blizzard.

Leonie began to cry, tears freezing on her cheeks. She tried to talk, but the angry wind tossed her words away. "Don't cry, Leonie." Betty clung to her sister, attempting to comfort her, but she was frightened too. She had lost all sense of direction and had no idea where the house was. Were they going to freeze here?

"Hey!" a male voice unexpectedly pierced the silence. "You two need help! Hop on the sled and hang on tight—I'll get you home!"

Who was it? Whirling snow made it impossible to see. "But you don't know where our house is," Betty called. Hadn't their father warned them about going with strangers?

"Sure I do!" he shouted back.

Why, it was Joe, Joe Martin! Joyfully, Betty recognized the voice of the seventeen-year-old who lived a mile down their road, one of the kindest people they knew. How lucky to have met him on this out-of-the-way hill!

"Get on the sled," Joe told them again, and both girls obeyed. They could just make out his tall silhouette as he bent to pick up the rope. Then they were off, clinging to each other as Joe pulled them across the fields.

Without his guidance, they surely would have missed the light from their kitchen window—even familiar markers were blurred and confusing in the whirling snow. But Joe stopped right at the back door. "You're home," he called over the gusts, hardly out of breath. "Jump off and get inside."

"Come in and get warm, Joe," Betty called as she waded through the drifts.

But no one answered. Joe was already gone.

A few days later, the girls went with their father to the Martin house. Mrs. Martin welcomed them, led them down the hall, then opened a door. Everyone looked inside.

Joe lay in bed, pale and tired. Had he caught a cold during the storm? Betty wondered.

"Joe, I came to thank you for taking such good care of my daughters," Betty's father told him.

Joe and his mother looked confused.

"The night before last, Joe," Betty prompted, "when you found us and brought us home."

"Nobody in his right mind would have gone out in that storm," Mrs. Martin protested, "especially Joe."

"But—"

"You see, he's been very ill with the flu," she went on, as Joe nodded weakly. "I've been at his bedside almost every moment. He hasn't been out of this room, much less outside, for the past week."

Betty and Leonie never discovered how Joe Martin managed to be in two places at once. But it was a gift they gladly accepted. Christmas was over—but God had saved the best present for last.

Into the Arms
of an Angel

Anyone who doesn't believe in miracles is not a realist.

DAVID BEN-GURION, PRIME MINISTER OF ISRAEL

O n October 24, 1993, five-year-old Paul Rosen fell out the window of his sixth-floor apartment on New York's East Side, landed on concrete—yet sustained no external or internal injuries. "Amazed paramedics, accustomed to removing a body from such accidents, instead treated a very-much-alive little boy," reported New York's *Daily News.* Said a medical technician, "It was like the angels caught him."

Many readers also told stories of God suspending the laws of gravity. Several years ago, Janet Dean was thoroughly cleaning the master bedroom on the second floor of her Wenonah, New Jersey, home. "I'd stripped the bed, and taken the screen off our window to hang the blankets out and shake them," she says. There was a lightweight wicker chair in front of the window, which Janet had not yet moved.

Just then Janet's two-and-a-half-year-old daughter, Debra, dashed into the room. Debra was a bundle of energy, always moving at a fast pace, curious and bouncy. The toddler sped by Janet and jumped up onto the wicker chair. It tipped backward and, in horror, Janet saw Debra plunge headfirst out of the second-story window.

"God, help!" Janet heard herself scream as Debra's feet slipped past her view.

Instantly, Debra's feet seemed to stop in midair. There was a momentary—and impossible—pause. Then, Janet says, "as if a camera had just been reversed, Debra came back through the window, feetfirst, and ended up standing on the chair."

"Oh, Debra!" Janet grabbed her little girl and held her close. She had seen it, she knew she had. Debra was proof of the miracle. But how? And why?

"I've stopped wondering about it," she says today. "I just give thanks."

Jerry, an experienced tree trimmer, shared his story with KKAR listeners in Omaha. One day he was about thirty or forty feet up in a tree, sitting on a long branch while using a chain saw to cut smaller shoots around him. "I should have been more careful," Jerry admitted, "but I hadn't thoroughly checked the limb I was sitting on." Suddenly he heard a cracking sound. The branch gave way, and Jerry started to fall, faceup, still holding the buzzing saw in front of him.

Options flew through his mind as he plummeted. Should he drop the saw? What if it hit a worker on the ground? Could he toss it away? No, it was too heavy, and the lethal blades might cut him if he tried. But if he held the saw, the impact would cause it to land on him anyway. "It seems odd that I weighed all those consequences during this brief fall," Jerry said. But since the fall itself would probably kill him, he decided to do nothing at all.

Jerry hit the ground. But it felt as if he had fallen into a big nest of pillows rather than on a hard surface. Just a little bounce, then—nothing, almost as if hands had cushioned the impact. Astonished, he lay there for a moment, then slowly got to his feet. Nothing broken, nothing even bruised. His astounded coworkers stood around him as he took a tentative step or two.

Then Jerry remembered the deadly tool he had been holding. Where was the chain saw?

He found it a moment later by following the sound of its still-whirring blades. It had landed harmlessly in an empty area across the yard, much too far for any man to throw it. And no one on the ground had seen it arc.

Jerry climbed the tree and resumed work a few moments later. But he hasn't stopped talking about what *might* have happened—if heavenly hands hadn't been nearby.

Clair told listeners on KYBG in Denver about a day when he, his wife, their two preschoolers, and infant were traveling. "Everyone was belted except the baby, who was lying in a bassinet on the backseat," Clair explained. "We shouldn't have put her there, but we just weren't thinking."

On a busy road, Clair lost control of the station wagon. It turned over twice, then came to a stop right side up. Dazed, Clair looked first at his wife, who seemed to be all right. Then he turned to check the children—and cried out in horror. His preschoolers were still belted, apparently unharmed. The bassinet was on the floor. But the wagon's tailgate had come open during the crash—and through it, Clair could see the baby lying in the middle of the street.

"My first thought was that the baby was dead and I had to pick her up before my wife did," Clair explained. He threw open the door and began racing, racing. . . . People were standing by the side of the street, all looking at the baby. Why didn't someone hold her? Why was she still there on the cement, so cold, so still? A sob rose in his throat.

But as Clair reached his daughter, he saw that there was no need for tears. The baby was lying on the concrete with nothing underneath her. But she was smiling, cooing, waving her arms—without even a bruise to mark her fall.

Then he realized why the witnesses had hesitated to touch her. "It was a miracle," each of them told him. "The baby came sailing through the open tailgate, at least six or seven feet above the pavement!"

Then she had simply stopped in midair and floated gently down.

Margy and Jared Nesset were cattle ranchers outside of Lander, Wyoming. They had a permit that let them run cattle in the Wind River Mountains during the summer—twenty-two thousand acres of beautiful mountain scenery, with many open grassy areas. Once a week Jared and Margy would ride horseback to check on the herd and, when necessary, move them to another grazing range.

One day the couple rode along, enjoying the golden beauty of their surroundings. Suddenly, something spooked Margy's horse. He reared, sunfished (a back-and-forth bucking motion), and pitched her into the air.

Jared watched with dread. The terrain was rocky, and it appeared that Margy's foot was still caught in the stirrup. After she landed, she would be dragged roughly along before he could get to her, bruising and perhaps even breaking bones. "When a horse is dethroning you," Margy explains, "there's no painless way to hit the ground."

And then, it looked to Jared as if the entire scene was slowing down, like a television replay. The horse seemed to be pitching in slow motion, and Margy was going toward the ground in that same drawn-out rhythm, not catapulting, but almost *drifting*. Was he seeing things?

No. For Margy experienced the same phenomenon. "I felt as if I was being gently lowered. I didn't actually hit the ground—it was more like I was laid down." Because her foot was caught in the stirrup, the horse started to drag her, but inexplicably came to a slow-motion stop. She had no wounds except a little scrape on her elbow.

Amazed, Margy got up and went to her husband. "Did you see that?" she asked. Jared is the logical one in the family, and she assumed he could explain away her impressions.

But Jared couldn't. What he had seen supported Margy's perspective. Further, Jared sensed another dimension, as if he had witnessed something significant and special.

Several years have passed, but Margy can still relive the fall with utter clarity, "just like one remembers each detail in connection with Pearl Harbor day or the assassination of President Kennedy," she says.

Who provided the unseen help? When they shared the story with a friend who is a Congregational minister, he suggested it might have been their mentally retarded son, Michael, who was killed in a tractor accident at age nineteen. "Mike was very strong physically and he loved horses," Margy remembers. "And after helping him for nineteen years, it's exciting to contemplate a switch-around—him helping us from heaven." Or perhaps the unseen hands were those of an angel.

Whatever the answer, the incident changed Margy forever. "Now my faith bridges marvelous gaps, where proof is no longer necessary," she says. "What a beautiful new freedom!"

God Calling

*Open your ears and open your hearts and hear me
well. You have never been forsaken. Nor was God
far away from you, even in your darkest hour. . . .*

JOSEPH F. GIRZONE, *JOSHUA*

*I*t had always been Ken Gaub's goal to help those who were
hurting. "Some people just need a little boost, and I wanted to
influence their lives in a positive way," he says. He became a
traveling missionary and, with his family, conducted crusades
not only throughout America but in many foreign countries.
He established a magazine, a radio and television ministry, a
youth outreach program.

But sometimes even preachers get drained and discouraged,
and they wonder if they should consider another line of work.
That was how Ken felt one day in the 1970s as he, his wife,
Barbara, and their children drove their two ministry buses
down I-75 just south of Dayton, Ohio. *God, am I doing any
good, traveling around like this, telling people about You?* he
wondered silently. *Is this what You want me to do?*

"Hey, Dad, let's get some pizza!" one of Ken's sons suggested. Still lost in thought, Ken turned off at the next exit, Route 741, where one sign after another advertised a wide variety of fast food. *A sign,* Ken mused. *That's what I need, God, a sign.*

Ken's son and daughter-in-law had already maneuvered the second bus into a pizza parlor's parking lot, and they stood waiting as Ken pulled up. The rest of the family bounced down the steps. Ken sat staring into space.

"Coming?" Barbara asked.

"I'm not really hungry," Ken told her. "I'll stay out here and stretch my legs."

Barbara followed the others into the restaurant, and Ken stepped outside, closed the bus doors, and looked around. Noticing a Dairy Queen, he strolled over, bought a soft drink, and ambled back, still pondering. He was exhausted. But were his doldrums a sign of permanent burnout?

A persistent ringing broke Ken's concentration. The jangle was coming from a pay telephone in a booth at the service station right next to the Dairy Queen. As Ken approached the booth, he looked to see if anyone in the station was coming to answer the phone. But the attendant continued his work, seemingly oblivious to the noise.

Why didn't someone answer it? Ken wondered, growing irritated. What if it was an emergency?

The insistent ringing went on. Ten rings. Fifteen. . . .

Curiosity overcame Ken's lethargy. Walking to the booth, he lifted the receiver. "Hello?"

"Long-distance call for Ken Gaub," came the voice of the operator.

Ken was stunned. "You're crazy!" he said. Then, realizing his rudeness, he tried to explain. "This can't be! I was just walking down the road here, and the phone was ringing—"

The operator ignored his ramblings. "Is Ken Gaub there?" she asked. "I have a long-distance phone call for him."

Was this a joke? Automatically, Ken smoothed his hair for the "Candid Camera" crew that must surely appear. But no one came. His family was eating pizza in a randomly selected restaurant just a few yards from where he stood. And no one else knew he was here.

"I have a long-distance call for Ken Gaub, sir," the operator said again, obviously reaching the limits of her patience. "Is he there or isn't he?"

"Operator, I'm Ken Gaub," Ken said, still unable to make sense of it.

"Are you sure?" the operator asked, but just then, Ken heard another woman's voice on the telephone.

"Yes, that's him, Operator!" she said. "Mr. Gaub, I'm Millie from Harrisburg, Pennsylvania. You don't know me, but I'm desperate. Please help me."

"What can I do for you?" Ken asked. The operator hung up.

Millie began to weep, and Ken waited patiently for her to regain control. Finally she explained: "I was about to kill myself, and I started to write a suicide note. Then I began to pray and tell God I really didn't want to do this." Through her desolation, Millie remembered seeing Ken on television. If she could just talk to that nice, kindly minister, the one with the understanding attitude. . . .

"I knew it was impossible because I didn't know how to reach you," Millie went on, calmer now. "So I started to finish the note. And then some numbers came into my mind, and I wrote them down." She began to weep again. Silently Ken prayed for the wisdom to help her.

"I looked at those numbers," Millie continued tearfully, "and I thought—wouldn't it be wonderful if I had a miracle from

God, and He has given me Ken's phone number? I can't believe I'm talking to you. Are you in your office in California?"

"I don't have an office in California," Ken explained. "It's in Yakima, Washington."

"Then where are you?" Millie asked, puzzled.

Ken was even more bewildered. "Millie, don't you know? You made the call."

"But I don't know what area this is." Millie had dialed the long-distance operator and given the numbers to her, making it a person-to-person call. And somehow she had found Ken in a parking lot in Dayton, Ohio.

Ken gently counseled the woman. Soon she met the One who would lead her out of her situation into a new life. Then he hung up the phone, still dazed. Would his family believe this incredible story? Perhaps he shouldn't tell anyone about it.

But he had prayed for an answer, and he had received just what he needed—a renewed sense of purpose, a glimpse of the value of his work, an electrifying awareness of God's concern for each of His children—all in an encounter that could only have been arranged by His heavenly Father.

Ken's heart overflowed with joy. "Barb," he exclaimed as his wife climbed back into the bus. "You won't believe this! God knows where I am!"[13]

≈ ≈

ANOTHER BEGINNING

Epilogue

I know not where lies Eden-land;
I only know 'tis like unto
God's kingdom, ever right at hand—
Ever right here in reach of you.

JOAQUIN MILLER,
"WITH LOVE TO YOU AND YOURS"

Our lives are filled with miracles. They begin with our very birth. For we are all God's children, each a special creation. "I have summoned you by name; you are mine," God tells us in Isaiah 43:1.

We seem to start life knowing and accepting this great comfort. Watch infants and toddlers as they respond to their world. For them, every moment is a miracle of joy, of wonder and discovery.

But something happens to us along the way. We become so involved with the business of living that we often lose sight of the Author of life, His plan for us, the miracles that He sends to us—beginning with the dawning of each new day. Life gets tough, and things don't always work out as we hoped. Sometimes we wonder if God is even there.

Yet it is at those very times of bleakness and discouragement that—if we're willing—we can create our own miracles of love and warmth and caring:

We can reach out beyond ourselves to touch the lives of others.

We can seek the hopeful in difficult situations and try to build on it.

We can risk rejection and offer help where we see it is needed.

We can honor our commitments.

We can forgive, as we would want to be forgiven.

We can love one another, even when there may be times when we cannot see the good that love will do.

We can travel through life, acting on the outside the way we want to feel on the inside, determined that when our journey is over, we will leave the world just a little better than we found it.

And as we reach out to one another in faith, something wonderful will surely happen. For we will find that we are also reaching *up*, to God—and that God is reaching *down*, to us, part of all the good we do, as close as a whispered prayer.

Not ancient faraway happenings, but here, today, now—like God's love, miracles are all around us. Just as they always have been. Just as they always will be.

Notes

1. Mary Ellen Strote, "The Power of Prayer," *Men's Fitness,* October 1992, p. 114.
2. Since this episode, hospital signs have been erected in Rock Springs.
3. Andrea Gross, "I Met an Angel," *Ladies' Home Journal,* December 1992, pp. 62–63.
4. Joy Snell, *The Ministry of Angels Here and Beyond* (New York: Citadel Press, 1959), p. 52.
5. To receive information or to enroll a chronically ill child, age four through twenty-one, in Love Letters (the service is free), contact Linda Bremner at Love Letters, P.O. Box 416875, Chicago, IL 60641-6875.
6. Betty Malz, *Angels Watching Over Me* (Old Tappan, NJ: Chosen Books, 1986), p. 113.
7. Charles and Frances Hunter, *Supernatural Horizons: From Glory to Glory* (Kingwood, TX: Hunter Books, 1983), p. 170.
8. For information on Teresa Griffin's book for bereaved parents, *Letters of Hope: Living After the Loss of Your Child,* write to: Cedarbrook Press, P.O. Box 2, Richboro, PA 18954.
9. Material taken from *Miracles Do Happen* by Sister Briege McKenna (Ann Arbor, MI: Servant Publications, 1987).

10. Richard Slade's cancer was not discovered earlier because it required a CAT scan for verification, a procedure usually not performed during routine physical examinations. Some physicians advise Vietnam veterans who believe they may have been exposed to Agent Orange to have a CAT scan annually.

11. For information on St. Michael of the Saints, novena leaflets, and medals, write to: The Trinitarians, P.O. Box 5719, Department M, Baltimore, MD 21208.

12. Material taken from *Miracles in El Paso?* by Rene Laurenten (Ann Arbor, MI: Servant Publications, 1982).

13. Ken Gaub's new book, *Dreams, Plans and Goals,* is published by New Leaf Press, Green Forest, AR. For information on Ken Gaub's ministries and speaking engagements, or to order his book ($10, postage paid), write to him at P.O. Box 1, Yakima, WA 98907.

Bibliography
and Additional Reading

AFTERLIFE

Eadie, Betty. *Embraced by the Light*. Placerville, CA: Gold Leaf Press, 1992.

Komp, Diane, M.D. *A Window to Heaven*. Grand Rapids: Zondervan Publishing House, 1992.

Morse, Melvin, M.D., with Paul Perry. *Transformed by the Light*. New York: Villard Books, 1992.

Patterson, Joy Davis. *Deathbed Miracles*. Nashville: Winston-Derek Publishers (Pennywell Drive, P.O. Box 90883, Nashville, TN 37209), 1991.

ANGELS

Freeman, Eileen. *Touched by Angels*. New York: Warner Books, 1993.

Graham, Billy. *Angels: God's Secret Agents*. New York: Doubleday, 1975.

Moolenburgh, H. C. *A Handbook of Angels*. Saffron Walden, England: C. W. Daniel Company (1 Church Path, Saffron Walden, Essex, CB10 1JP, England), 1988.

———. *Meetings with Angels*. Saffron Walden, England: C. W. Daniel Company, 1992.

Webber, Marilynn and William. *The Rustle of Angels*. Grand Rapids: Zondervan Publishing House, 1994.

HEALING

DiOrio, Father Ralph A. *A Miracle to Proclaim*. Tarrytown, NY: Triumph Books, 1991.
Schiappacasse, Chuck. *God Heals Today*. Glenview, IL: C. Schiappacasse, 1993.
Siegel, Bernie S., M.D. *Love, Medicine & Miracles*. New York: Harper & Row, 1986.
Wolpe, Rabbi David J. *The Healer of Shattered Hearts: A Jewish View of God*. New York: Henry Holt & Company, 1990.

MIRACLES

Bredesen, Harald, with James F. Scheer. *Need a Miracle?*. Grand Rapids: Fleming H. Revell Company, 1979.
DeGrandis, Father Robert, S.S.J., with Linda Schubert. *The Gift of Miracles*. Ann Arbor, MI: Servant Publications, 1991.
Huyssen, Chester and Lucile. *I Saw the Lord*. Tarrytown, NY: Chosen Books, 1977.

AUTHOR'S AFTERWORD

I am always interested in hearing from people who have angel stories, healings, answers to prayer, and other heavenly experiences to share. Please write to me at P.O. Box 1694, Arlington Heights, IL 60006. I will keep your letter on file, and I will contact you if I find a place for your story in my future writing.

—J. W. A.